Chocolate Mousse, page 30

Cooking Light.

Dessert

Oxmoor House.

©2006 by Oxmoor House, Inc.
Book Division of Southern Progress Corporation
P.O. Box 2262, Birmingham, Alabama 35201

ISBN-13: 978-0-8487-3066-6
ISBN-10: 0-8487-3066-6
Library of Congress Control Number:
2006929983
Printed in the United States of America
First printing 2006

Be sure to check with your health-care provider
before making any changes in your diet.

Oxmoor House, Inc.
Editor in Chief: Nancy Fitzpatrick Wyatt
Executive Editor: Katherine M. Eakin
Copy Chief: Allison Long Lowery

Cooking Light® Dessert
Editor: Heather Averett
Copy Editor: Diane Rose
Editorial Assistant: Julie Boston
Nutrition Editorial Assistant:
    Rachel Quinlivan, R.D.
Photography Director: Jim Bathie
Senior Photo Stylist: Kay E. Clarke
Photo Stylist: Katherine Eckert
Director, Test Kitchens: Elizabeth Tyler Austin
Assistant Director, Test Kitchens:
    Julie Christopher
Test Kitchens Staff: Nicole Lee Faber,
    Kathleen Royal Phillips
Food Stylist: Kelley Self Wilton
Director of Production: Laura Lockhart
Senior Production Manager: Greg A. Amason
Production Manager: Tamara Nall
Production Assistant: Faye Porter Bonner

Contributors:
Designer: Carol Damsky
Indexer: Mary Ann Laurens
Editorial Interns: Jill Baughman, Ashley Leath,
    Caroline Markunas, Mary Katherine Pappas,
    Vanessa Rusch Thomas, Lucas Whittington
Photographer: Beau Gustafson

To order additional publications, call
1-800-765-6400, or visit oxmoorhouse.com

CONTENTS

Essential Desserts   8

Chocolaty brownies, creamy banana
pudding, homemade apple pie—here
are our undeniably best-of-the best
must-have desserts. Perfected by *Cooking
Light,* these recipes are so good that only
the cook will know they're light.

Cookies & Bars   34

Go ahead—get caught with your hand
in the cookie jar. With these light bites,
reaching for a treat is a guilt-free
pleasure. Our lightened versions of
traditional-style oatmeal-raisin, peanut
butter, and sugar cookies will have you
coming back for more.

Cakes   52

Tender layer cakes; party-pleasing cupcakes; cool, creamy cheesecake—each
delectable treat is one of the sweetest
ways to end a meal.

Pies & Pastries   74

Whether it's a slice of classic, nutty pecan pie; a spoonful of homestyle peach cobbler; or a flaky, triangular apple-stuffed turnover, these pies and pastries will satisfy your sweet tooth and your conscience.

Fruit Desserts   96

Cut into an almond-stuffed baked apple drizzled with caramel-apple sauce, or spoon into a tropical sundae loaded with kiwi and mango. Whatever the season, fruit grants dessert a sweet head start.

Custards, Puddings & Soufflés   116

Creamy, comforting, and classic are the characteristics of these sophisticated yet simple desserts. Each one is a fitting finale to a delicious dinner.

Cooking Light®
Editor in Chief: Mary Kay Culpepper
Executive Editor: Billy R. Sims
Art Director: Susan Waldrip Dendy
Managing Editor: Maelynn Cheung
Senior Food Editor: Alison Mann Ashton
Features Editor: Phillip Rhodes
Projects Editor: Mary Simpson Creel, M.S., R.D.
Food Editor: Ann Taylor Pittman
Associate Food Editors: Julianna Grimes Bottcher,
    Timothy Q. Cebula
Assistant Food Editor: Kathy C. Kitchens, R.D.
Assistant Editors: Cindy Hatcher,
    Brandy Rushing
Test Kitchens Director: Vanessa Taylor Johnson
Senior Food Stylist: Kellie Gerber Kelley
Food Stylist: M. Kathleen Kanen
Test Kitchens Professionals: Sam Brannock,
    Kathryn Conrad, Mary H. Drennen,
    Jan Jacks Moon, Tiffany Vickers,
    Mike Wilson
Assistant Art Director: Maya Metz Logue
Senior Designers: Fernande Bondarenko,
    J. Shay McNamee
Designer: Brigette Mayer
Senior Photographer: Randy Mayor
Senior Photo Stylist: Cindy Barr
Photo Stylists: Melanie J. Clarke, Jan Gautro
Studio Assistant: Celine Chenoweth
Copy Chief: Maria Parker Hopkins
Senior Copy Editor: Susan Roberts
Copy Editor: Johannah Paiva
Production Manager: Liz Rhoades
Production Editors: Joanne McCrary Brasseal,
    Hazel R. Eddins
Administrative Coordinator: Carol D. Johnson
Office Manager: Rita K. Jackson
Editorial Assistant: Melissa Hoover
Correspondence Editor: Michelle Gibson Daniels
Interns: Sabrina Bone, Kimberly Burnstad,
    Melissa Marek, Molly Kate Matthews,
    Megan Voelkel

CookingLight.com
Editor: Jennifer Middleton Richards
Online Producer: Abigail Masters

Cover: *Strawberry Shortcake Jelly Roll (page 16)*

Welcome

Dessert is delectable, dreamy, and utterly delicious. But there's another thing that dessert is, and that's essential. For a *Cooking Light*® cook, dessert is divine and amazingly guilt-free.

In this cookbook, you'll find the dessert recipes we believe to be the essential recipes for every *Cooking Light* cook. These recipes are our tried-and-true classics—ones we love to make again and again.

Each chapter offers mouthwatering, flavorful recipes, complete with nutritional analyses that will help you eat smart, be fit, and live well. After all, eating smart, being fit, and living well are essential in our minds.

So whether you're looking for a down-home recipe for Blueberry Cobbler or for something with a little more panache, such as Classic Crème Caramel, you're sure to find it in this edition of *The Cooking Light Cook's Essential Recipe Collection*. I hope these recipes will become as essential to your family as they are to the *Cooking Light* family.

Very truly yours,

Mary Kay Culpepper
Editor in Chief

essential
desserts

Fudgy Mocha-Toffee Brownies

Cooking spray
2 tablespoons instant coffee
  granules
¼ cup hot water
¼ cup butter
¼ cup semisweet chocolate
  chips
1½ cups all-purpose flour
1⅓ cups sugar
½ cup unsweetened cocoa
1 teaspoon baking powder
½ teaspoon salt
1 teaspoon vanilla extract
2 large eggs, lightly beaten
¼ cup toffee chips

1. Preheat oven to 350°.
2. Coat bottom of a 9-inch square baking pan with cooking spray.
3. Combine coffee and hot water, stirring until coffee dissolves.
4. Combine butter and chocolate chips in a small microwave-safe bowl. Microwave at HIGH 1 minute or until butter melts; stir until chocolate is smooth.
5. Lightly spoon flour into dry measuring cups; level with a knife. Combine flour, sugar, cocoa, baking powder, and salt in a large bowl, stirring with a whisk. Combine coffee mixture, butter mixture, vanilla, and eggs in a medium bowl, stirring with a whisk. Add coffee mixture to flour mixture; stir just until combined. Spread evenly into prepared pan. Sprinkle evenly with toffee chips. Bake at 350° for 22 minutes. Cool on a wire rack. Yield: 16 servings.

CALORIES 179 (30% from fat); FAT 5.9g (sat 3.3g, mono 1.4g, poly 0.3g); PROTEIN 2.7g; CARB 30.7g; FIBER 1.4g; CHOL 36mg; IRON 1.2mg; SODIUM 149mg; CALC 28mg

Cocoa powder is made from ground roasted cacao seeds. It is the best choice for light baking because it delivers the richest chocolaty flavor with the least amount of fat. There are two types: natural (nonalkalized) and Dutch process (alkalized). Though both are unsweetened cocoa, their flavors differ slightly. Natural cocoa is tart and acidic, while Dutch process cocoa has a mellow toasted flavor. It's best to store cocoa in an airtight container away from herbs, spices, and other aromatic substances. It picks up other flavors easily.

Coffee and toffee give these rich, decadent chocolate brownies a unique twist. If they haven't all been gobbled up, store leftover brownies in an airtight container up to one week, or wrap them tightly in aluminum foil, and freeze up to four months.

Angel Food Cake

1 cup sifted cake flour
1¼ cups sugar, divided
10 egg whites
1¼ teaspoons cream of tartar
⅛ teaspoon salt
⅛ teaspoon vanilla extract

1. Preheat oven to 350°.

2. Sift together flour and ¼ cup sugar; set aside. Beat egg whites with a mixer at high speed until foamy. Add cream of tartar and salt; beat until soft peaks form. Add remaining 1 cup sugar, 2 tablespoons at a time, beating until stiff peaks form. Sift ¼ cup flour mixture over egg white mixture, and fold in. Repeat procedure with remaining flour mixture, ¼ cup at a time. Fold in vanilla.

3. Spoon batter into an ungreased 10-inch tube pan, spreading evenly. Break air pockets by cutting through batter with a knife. Bake at 350° for 40 minutes or until cake springs back when lightly touched. Invert pan; cool 40 minutes. Loosen cake from sides of pan using a narrow metal spatula; invert cake onto a serving plate. Yield: 12 servings (serving size: 1 slice).

CALORIES 126 (0% from fat); FAT 0.1g (sat 0g, mono 0g, poly 0g); PROTEIN 3.5g; CARB 27.6g; FIBER 0.3g; CHOL 0mg; IRON 0.6mg; SODIUM 70mg; CALC 3mg

There are two key steps in making an angel food cake. Step one is beating the egg whites until they form stiff peaks. Step two is gradually folding the cake flour, ¼ cup at a time, into the beaten egg whites. Use a rubber spatula to gently fold the batter over and under until the flour and egg whites are combined. Beating the batter with a mixer will deflate the egg whites, and the cake will not rise to its full height.

Delicate angel food cake is naturally light because it's made with egg whites, while the yolks or other fats are omitted. In addition to enjoying the sweet taste and tender texture of an unadorned piece of angel food cake, try cutting it into cubes and layering it with pudding and fruit for a trifle. Or top it with berries or sliced fruit. And if you're feeling particularly indulgent, consider spooning warm caramel or chocolate sauce over a high-volume, spongy slice.

Sour Cream–Lemon Pound Cake

Beating softened butter until it's light and fluffy is a very important step in making a pound cake. It contributes to both the height and tenderness of the cake. It's important to start with softened butter, but this can be a tricky thing to judge. Let the butter sit at room temperature approximately 30 minutes before you're ready to begin the recipe. To make sure the butter is softened, lightly press on it with a clean fingertip. If it leaves an imprint, the butter is ready to use.

Cooking spray
  3 tablespoons dry breadcrumbs
3¼ cups all-purpose flour
  ½ teaspoon baking soda
  ¼ teaspoon salt
  ¾ cup butter, softened
2½ cups granulated sugar
  2 teaspoons lemon extract
  3 large eggs
1½ tablespoons grated lemon rind (about 2 lemons)
  ¼ cup fresh lemon juice, divided
  1 (8-ounce) carton low-fat sour cream
  1 cup powdered sugar
Fresh raspberries (optional)
Reduced-calorie whipped topping, thawed (optional)

1. Preheat oven to 350°.

2. Coat a 10-inch tube pan with cooking spray; dust with breadcrumbs.

3. Lightly spoon flour into dry measuring cups; level with a knife. Combine flour, baking soda, and salt in a bowl; stir well with a whisk. Place butter in a large bowl; beat with a mixer at medium speed until light and fluffy. Gradually add granulated sugar and lemon extract, beating until well blended. Add eggs, 1 at a time, beating well after each addition. Add grated lemon rind and 2 tablespoons lemon juice; beat 30 seconds. Add flour mixture to sugar mixture alternately with sour cream, beating at low speed, beginning and ending with flour mixture.

4. Spoon batter into prepared pan. Bake at 350° for 1 hour and 10 minutes or until a wooden pick inserted in center comes out clean. Cool in pan 10 minutes on a wire rack; remove from pan. Cool completely on rack. Combine remaining 2 tablespoons lemon juice and powdered sugar. Drizzle glaze over cake. Garnish with raspberries and whipped topping, if desired. Yield: 18 servings (serving size: 1 slice).

Note: For a Sour Cream Pound Cake variation, substitute vanilla extract for lemon extract. Omit lemon juice and rind in cake. Substitute milk for lemon juice in glaze.

CALORIES 323 (29% from fat); FAT 10.4g (sat 6g, mono 3g, poly 0.6g); PROTEIN 4g; CARB 53.4g; FIBER 0.7g; CHOL 62mg; IRON 1.3mg; SODIUM 172mg; CALC 27mg

Though it's thought to be of British origin, there's still much discrepancy today about the genesis of the pound cake. Regardless, the cake receives its name from the original ingredient measurements: a pound of sugar, a pound of flour, a pound of butter, and a pound of eggs. Thankfully, while the amounts of the ingredients have changed, this classic cake still remains a favorite.

Strawberry Shortcake Jelly Roll

4 cups sliced strawberries
(about 1½ pounds)
¾ cup granulated sugar,
divided
Cooking spray
⅔ cup all-purpose flour
1 teaspoon baking powder
¼ teaspoon salt
5 egg whites
3 egg yolks
2 teaspoons grated lemon rind
1 teaspoon vanilla extract
2 tablespoons powdered
sugar
1 (10-ounce) jar strawberry jam
½ cup whipping cream
Orange rind strips (optional)
Mint sprigs (optional)

At first glance, making a jelly-roll cake may seem complicated. But by closely following the recipe's instructions, this dessert is quite easy. All you'll need to prepare this simple cake is a shallow rectangular pan (jelly-roll pan) and a kitchen towel (such as a small, rectangular terry cloth towel or tea towel) to remove moisture and prevent sticking when rolling up the cake. After your cake has cooled for an hour while rolled up in the cloth, unroll it, spread the filling, and reroll (this time without the towel). Place the cake on a serving platter seam side down, slice, and enjoy!

1. Combine strawberries and ¼ cup granulated sugar in a medium bowl. Cover and chill; stir occasionally.
2. Preheat oven to 400°.
3. Coat a 15 x 10–inch jelly-roll pan with cooking spray, and line bottom of pan with wax paper. Coat wax paper with cooking spray.
4. Lightly spoon flour into dry measuring cups; level with a knife. Combine flour, baking powder, and salt, stirring with a whisk. Set aside.
5. Place remaining ½ cup granulated sugar, egg whites, and egg yolks in a large bowl; beat with a mixer at high speed until pale and fluffy (about 5 minutes). Stir in lemon rind and vanilla. Sift half of flour mixture over egg mixture; fold in. Repeat procedure with remaining flour mixture. Spoon batter into prepared pan; spread evenly.
6. Bake at 400° for 10 minutes or until cake springs back when touched lightly in center. Loosen cake from sides of pan; turn out onto a dish towel dusted with powdered sugar. Carefully peel off wax paper; cool cake 2 minutes. Starting at narrow end, roll up cake and towel together. Place, seam side down, on a wire rack; cool completely (about 1 hour). Unroll carefully; remove towel. Spread jam over cake, leaving a ½-inch border around edges. Reroll cake; place, seam side down, on a platter. Cut into 8 slices.
7. Beat cream with a mixer at high speed until soft peaks form. Serve strawberries and whipped cream with cake. Garnish with orange rind and mint sprigs, if desired. Yield: 8 servings (serving size: 1 cake slice, about ½ cup berries, and about 2 tablespoons whipped cream).

CALORIES 318 (22% from fat); FAT 7.6g (sat 4.1g, mono 2.4g, poly 0.6g); PROTEIN 5.2g; CARB 59.3g; FIBER 2g; CHOL 97mg; IRON 1.1mg; SODIUM 179mg; CALC 69mg

Usher in spring with this lovely dessert featuring fresh strawberries and whipped cream.

(pictured on cover)

New York Cheesecake

A springform pan—a round, deep pan with tall removable sides—is the most commonly used pan for baking cheesecakes. Springform pans with glass bottoms conduct heat better and decrease cooking time. If possible, use a springform pan with an extended edge around the base to keep the batter from leaking, or wrap the outside of the pan with aluminum foil. Because we wanted the height of a traditional New York–style cheesecake, we baked this in a springform pan with high (3-inch) sides. If you're not sure about the dimensions of your pan, use a ruler to measure the inside of the pan.

Crust:
- ⅔ cup all-purpose flour
- 3 tablespoons sugar
- 2 tablespoons chilled butter, cut into small pieces
- 1 tablespoon ice water
- Cooking spray

Filling:
- 4 cups fat-free cottage cheese
- 2 cups sugar
- 2 (8-ounce) blocks ⅓-less-fat cream cheese, softened
- ¼ cup all-purpose flour
- ½ cup fat-free sour cream
- 1 tablespoon grated lemon rind
- 1 tablespoon vanilla extract
- ¼ teaspoon salt
- 5 large eggs

1. Preheat oven to 400°.

2. To prepare crust, lightly spoon ⅔ cup flour into dry measuring cups; level with a knife. Place ⅔ cup flour and 3 tablespoons sugar in a food processor; pulse 2 times or until combined. Add butter; pulse 6 times or until mixture resembles coarse meal. With processor on, slowly pour ice water through food chute, processing just until blended (do not allow dough to form a ball).

3. Firmly press mixture into bottom of a 9 x 3–inch springform pan coated with cooking spray. Bake at 400° for 10 minutes or until lightly browned; cool on a wire rack.

4. Reduce oven temperature to 325°.

5. To prepare filling, strain cottage cheese through a cheesecloth-lined sieve 10 minutes; discard liquid. Place cottage cheese in food processor; process until smooth.

6. Place 2 cups sugar and cream cheese in a large bowl; beat with a mixer at medium speed until smooth. Lightly spoon ¼ cup flour into a dry measuring cup; level with a knife. Add ¼ cup flour, sour cream, and next 4 ingredients to cream cheese mixture; beat well. Add cottage cheese, stirring until well blended. Pour cheese mixture into prepared crust.

7. Bake at 325° for 1½ hours or until almost set. Turn oven off. Cool cheesecake in closed oven 1 hour. Remove cheesecake from oven; run a knife around outside edge. Cool to room temperature. Cover and chill at least 8 hours. Yield: 16 servings (serving size: 1 wedge).

Note: You can also make cheesecake in a 10 x 2½–inch springform pan. Bake at 300° for 1½ hours or until almost set. Turn oven off. Cool cheesecake in closed oven 30 minutes.

CALORIES 291 (30% from fat); FAT 9.8g (sat 5.7g, mono 3g, poly 0.5g); PROTEIN 12.9g; CARB 37.7g; FIBER 0.2g; CHOL 98mg; IRON 0.7mg; SODIUM 410mg; CALC 93mg

Double-Crusted Apple Pie

This adaptable piecrust is worth the effort to make. It's easy, it tastes great, and it has about half the fat of the full-fat version. When rolling out the dough, follow a north, south, east, and west motion, lifting up the rolling pin as you near the edges to prevent them from becoming too thin. Handle the dough as little as possible, and after rolling it out, place it in the freezer for 5 minutes. Then invert it into the pie plate, and peel off the plastic wrap.

Pastry:
2½ cups all-purpose flour
  ½ teaspoon salt
  ½ cup vegetable shortening
  ½ cup ice water
Cooking spray

Filling:
  10 cups thinly sliced peeled
      Granny Smith apple (about
      3 pounds)
  ¾ cup granulated sugar
1½ tablespoons all-purpose
      flour
  1 teaspoon ground cinnamon
  ½ teaspoon salt
  ¼ teaspoon ground nutmeg
  1 tablespoon chilled butter,
      cut into small pieces

Topping:
  1 tablespoon fat-free milk
  1 teaspoon turbinado sugar

1. To prepare pastry, lightly spoon 2½ cups flour into dry measuring cups; level with a knife. Combine 2½ cups flour and ½ teaspoon salt in a large bowl. Stir well with a whisk; cut in shortening with a pastry blender or 2 knives until mixture resembles coarse meal. Gradually add ice water; toss with a fork until flour mixture is moist. Divide dough into 2 equal portions. Gently press each portion into a 4-inch circle on heavy-duty plastic wrap; cover and chill 30 minutes.

2. Slightly overlap 2 sheets of plastic wrap on a slightly damp surface. Unwrap and place 1 portion of chilled dough on plastic wrap. Cover dough with 2 additional sheets of overlapping plastic wrap. Roll dough, still covered, into a 12-inch circle. Place dough in freezer 5 minutes or until plastic wrap can be easily removed. Remove top sheets of plastic wrap; fit dough, plastic wrap side up, into a 9-inch deep-dish pie plate coated with cooking spray. Remove remaining plastic wrap.

3. Preheat oven to 425°.

4. To prepare filling, combine apple and next 5 ingredients, and toss gently to coat. Spoon apple mixture into prepared pie plate; top with butter.

5. Roll remaining portion of dough into an 11-inch circle, repeating procedure from Step 2, including freezing dough. Remove top sheets of plastic wrap; fit dough, plastic wrap side up, over apple mixture. Remove remaining plastic wrap. Press edges of dough together. Fold edges under, and flute. Cut several slits in top of dough to allow steam to escape.

6. To prepare topping, brush top of dough with milk; sprinkle turbinado sugar evenly over dough. Place pie plate on a foil-lined baking sheet; bake at 425° for 10 minutes. Reduce oven temperature to 350° (do not remove pie from oven); bake an additional 40 minutes or until browned. Cool on a wire rack. Yield: 10 servings (serving size: 1 wedge).

CALORIES 333 (30% from fat); FAT 11.2g (sat 3.1g, mono 3.7g, poly 2.6g); PROTEIN 3.7g; CARB 55.2g; FIBER 2.5g; CHOL 3mg; IRON 1.7mg; SODIUM 245mg; CALC 15mg

Blueberry Cobbler

For tender, flaky pastry, use a pastry blender or a pair of knives to cut the chilled butter into the flour. The blades of the pastry blender quickly combine the butter and flour, forming a dry mixture that resembles coarse meal. If using two knives, hold a knife in each hand. Then pull the knives in opposite directions with the blades passing close together through the butter and flour.

Filling:
- 6 cups fresh blueberries
- 1/3 cup sugar
- 2 tablespoons cornstarch
- 1 teaspoon grated lemon rind

Topping:
- 1 1/3 cups all-purpose flour
- 2 tablespoons sugar
- 3/4 teaspoon baking powder
- 1/4 teaspoon salt
- 1/4 teaspoon baking soda
- 5 tablespoons chilled butter, cut into small pieces
- 1 cup fat-free sour cream
- 3 tablespoons 2% reduced-fat milk
- 1 teaspoon sugar

1. Preheat oven to 350°.
2. To prepare filling, combine first 4 ingredients in an 11 x 7–inch baking dish.
3. To prepare topping, lightly spoon flour into dry measuring cups, and level with a knife. Combine flour and next 4 ingredients in a large bowl, stirring with a whisk. Cut in butter with a pastry blender or 2 knives until mixture resembles coarse meal. Stir in sour cream to form a soft dough.
4. Drop dough by spoonfuls onto blueberry filling to form 8 dumplings. Brush dumplings with milk; sprinkle with 1 teaspoon sugar. Place baking dish on a jelly-roll pan. Bake at 350° for 50 minutes or until filling is bubbly and dumplings are lightly browned. Yield: 8 servings.

CALORIES 288 (26% from fat); FAT 8.3g (sat 4.9g, mono 2.2g, poly 0.5g); PROTEIN 4.7g; CARB 50.8g; FIBER 3.5g; CHOL 23mg; IRON 1.3mg; SODIUM 265mg; CALC 90mg

Beginning as a spin on pies, cobblers date back to the 1850s. The traditional New England concoction used a thick biscuit topping instead of pie pastry. While variations abound, a traditional cobbler is a baked deep-dish fruit dessert that's topped with a biscuit crust and sprinkled with sugar to give it a bit of crunch and color.

Simple Peach Ice Cream

6 cups sliced peeled peaches
(about 3 pounds)
¾ cup sugar
2 cups half-and-half
1½ teaspoons vanilla extract
¼ teaspoon salt

1. Combine peaches and sugar in a large bowl. Let stand 30 minutes, stirring occasionally. Place peach mixture in a food processor; pulse 10 times or until coarsely chopped. Return peach mixture to bowl, and stir in half-and-half, vanilla, and salt.

2. Pour mixture into the freezer can of an ice-cream freezer; freeze according to manufacturer's instructions. Spoon ice cream into a freezer-safe container; cover and freeze 1 hour or until firm. Yield: 12 servings (serving size: ½ cup).

CALORIES 138 (31% from fat); FAT 4.7g (sat 2.9g, mono 1.4g, poly 0.2g); PROTEIN 1.8g; CARB 23.7g; FIBER 1.7g; CHOL 15mg; IRON 0.1mg; SODIUM 65mg; CALC 46mg

It's important not to skip the first step in this recipe. Allowing the peaches and sugar to stand at room temperature for 30 minutes brings out the distinct taste of the peaches and creates a syrup that enhances the flavor of the ice cream. If your peaches are perfectly ripe, a potato masher will coarsely chop the peaches just as well as a food processor.

Summer is the time for cannonball contests, grilled burgers, and lightweight novels. To add to the fun, slice some fragrant, ripe peaches, and make this homemade ice cream. With a short list of natural ingredients and a no-cook method, it's ready to freeze quickly. Use an old-fashioned ice-cream freezer, or try the newer kind that needs no ice or salt. Either way, you'll wish that summer would never end.

Banana Pudding

⅓ cup all-purpose flour
Dash of salt
2½ cups 1% low-fat milk
1 (14-ounce) can fat-free sweetened condensed milk
2 large egg yolks
2 teaspoons vanilla extract
3 cups sliced ripe banana
45 reduced-fat vanilla wafers
4 large egg whites (at room temperature)
¼ cup sugar

1. Preheat oven to 325°.

2. Lightly spoon flour into a dry measuring cup; level with a knife. Combine flour and salt in a medium saucepan. Gradually add milks and egg yolks; stir well. Cook over medium heat, stirring constantly, until thick, about 8 to 10 minutes. Remove from heat; stir in vanilla.

3. Arrange 1 cup banana slices in bottom of a 2-quart baking dish. Spoon one-third of pudding mixture over banana slices in dish. Arrange 15 wafers on top of pudding. Repeat layers twice, arranging the last 15 wafers around edge of dish. Push wafers into pudding.

4. Beat egg whites with a mixer at high speed until foamy. Gradually add sugar, 1 tablespoon at a time, beating until stiff peaks form. Spread meringue evenly over pudding, sealing to cookies around edge of dish. Bake at 325° for 25 minutes or until golden. Yield: 10 servings (serving size: ¾ cup).

Note: Banana Pudding may be a bit soupy when you first remove it from the oven. Let it cool at least 30 minutes before serving.

CALORIES 255 (10% from fat); FAT 2.9g (sat 1g, mono 0.9g, poly 0.2g); PROTEIN 7.9g; CARB 49.5g; FIBER 0.1g; CHOL 51mg; IRON 0.4mg; SODIUM 155mg; CALC 161mg

Although it costs much less, don't be tempted to substitute imitation vanilla extract for pure vanilla extract. Pure vanilla is one of the most complex tastes in the world. There's no mistaking the unique flavor and aroma of this brown liquid that's extracted from the vanilla bean. Imitation vanilla extract is artificially created from chemicals and lacks the depth of flavor of the real thing.

No one knows the origin of banana pudding, but it has been a favorite American dessert for decades. If you grew up in the South, chances are the recipe was a part of your grandmother's or mother's repertoire. With its creamy vanilla-banana filling, mile-high meringue peaks, and chewy cookie "crust," it just begs for you to dig in.

Classic Crème Caramel

⅓ cup sugar
3 tablespoons water
Cooking spray
3 large eggs
1 large egg white
2 cups 2% reduced-fat milk
1 tablespoon vanilla extract
⅔ cup sugar
⅛ teaspoon salt
Fresh raspberries (optional)

Creating the wonderfully sweet caramel that sits atop this light custard isn't difficult if you give a little attention to the timing. Once the sugar dissolves into the water in the saucepan, refrain from stirring the mixture until it starts to turn brown. This means the mixture is beginning to caramelize. Once the mixture has turned golden (in about 1 to 2 minutes), immediately pour enough caramel to coat the bottom of each ramekin or custard cup. Then tilt each cup so that the caramel evenly covers the bottom of each cup. After that, you're ready to fill each cup with the custard mixture.

1. Preheat oven to 325°.
2. Combine ⅓ cup sugar and 3 tablespoons water in a small, heavy saucepan over medium-high heat; cook until sugar dissolves, stirring frequently. Continue cooking 4 minutes or until golden. Immediately pour into 6 (6-ounce) ramekins or custard cups coated with cooking spray, tilting each cup quickly until caramelized sugar coats bottom of cup. Set aside.
3. Beat eggs and egg white with a whisk. Stir in milk, vanilla, ⅔ cup sugar, and salt. Divide mixture evenly among custard cups. Place cups in a 13 x 9–inch baking pan; add hot water to pan to a depth of 1 inch. Bake at 325° for 45 minutes or until a knife inserted in center comes out clean. Remove cups from pan. Cover and chill at least 4 hours.
4. Loosen edges of custards with a thin, sharp knife. Place a dessert plate, upside down, on top of each cup; invert onto plates. Drizzle remaining syrup over custards. Garnish with raspberries, if desired. Yield: 6 servings.

CALORIES 212 (18% from fat); FAT 4.3g (sat 1.8g, mono 1.5g, poly 0.4g); PROTEIN 6.5g; CARB 37.6g; FIBER 0g; CHOL 117mg; IRON 0.4mg; SODIUM 131mg; CALC 113mg

Ever felt a silky-smooth, sweet spoonful of crème caramel glide along your tongue and melt inside your mouth? The experience is unforgettable. Despite the eternal allure of this classic dessert, it carries the reputation of being difficult to make. Some find the water-bath step somewhat intimidating, but here are a few tips that will help: Place your 13 x 9–inch pan containing the ramekins on the oven rack first, and then pour the hot water to a depth of 1 inch using a large measuring cup. Then, when removing the ramekins from the water bath, consider using jar grippers, which are sold with canning supplies, or use a pancake turner and balance the ramekins with an oven mitt.

Chocolate Mousse

¾ cup semisweet chocolate
    chips, melted
1 (12.3-ounce) package
    reduced-fat extrafirm silken
    tofu (such as Mori-Nu)
¼ teaspoon salt
3 large egg whites
½ cup sugar
¼ cup water
Fat-free whipped topping,
    thawed (optional)
Grated chocolate (optional)

1. Place melted chocolate chips and tofu in a food proces-sor or blender, and process 2 minutes or until smooth.
2. Place salt and egg whites in a medium bowl, and beat with a mixer at high speed until stiff peaks form. Combine sugar and water in a small saucepan; bring to a boil. Cook, without stirring, until a candy thermometer registers 250°. Pour hot sugar syrup in a thin stream over egg whites, beat-ing at high speed. Gently stir one-fourth of meringue into tofu mixture; gently fold in remaining meringue. Spoon ½ cup mousse into each of 8 (6-ounce) custard cups. Cover and chill at least 4 hours. Garnish with whipped topping and grated chocolate, if desired. Yield: 8 servings.

CALORIES 147 (34% from fat); FAT 5.6g (sat 3.3g, mono 1.8g, poly 0.5g); PROTEIN 5.2g; CARB 22.5g; FIBER 0.2g; CHOL 0mg; IRON 0.9mg; SODIUM 134mg; CALC 26mg

When tofu is whirled in the food processor or blender, it becomes smooth and creamy without the gritty or grainy consistency that low-fat dairy products can sometimes have. After its transformation, it becomes a peerless base for smooth-textured sweets. And because of its mildness, tofu doesn't get in the way of more traditional flavors, such as chocolate, rum, butterscotch, and vanilla. But tofu's crowning achievement is its role in this chocolate mousse, which our food staff unanimously awarded its highest rating.

Tofu is incredible at masquerading as a creamy dairy product in nearly any dessert, including chocolate mousse. We found this out firsthand in our Test Kitchens, where even the tofu skeptics acknowledged defeat when they tasted this sinfully delicious dessert. And the best part of this treat is that it contains two ingredients most women want more of: soy and chocolate.

Chocolate Soufflés with Pistachios

Ramekins and custard cups can often be used interchangeably, as they are both small ovenproof dishes that offer individual portions. Ramekins are generally made of porcelain or earthenware, while custard cups are made of tempered glass. Ramekins and custard cups come in various sizes, and it's important to use the ounce size called for in the recipe. The ounce size should be indicated on the bottom of the container. If not, fill the container with water; then pour the water into a liquid measuring cup. The level of the water will tell you the ounce size of the container.

Cooking spray
7 tablespoons plus 1 teaspoon sugar, divided
1½ tablespoons butter
1 ounce semisweet chocolate
2 tablespoons unsweetened cocoa
2 tablespoons all-purpose flour
⅛ teaspoon salt
½ cup 1% low-fat milk
3 large egg whites
4 teaspoons chopped pistachio nuts

1. Preheat oven to 375°.
2. Coat 4 (6-ounce) ramekins or custard cups with cooking spray, and dust each with 1 teaspoon sugar. Place on a baking sheet.
3. Combine 3 tablespoons sugar, butter, and chocolate in a small saucepan. Cook over low heat until melted. Add cocoa, flour, and salt, stirring with a whisk until blended. Gradually stir in milk, and cook over medium heat until mixture thickens (about 3 minutes), stirring constantly. Remove from heat. Cool.
4. Beat egg whites with a mixer at high speed until foamy. Add remaining 3 tablespoons sugar, 1 tablespoon at a time, beating until stiff peaks form. Gently fold one-fourth of egg white mixture into chocolate mixture; repeat procedure with remaining egg white mixture, one-fourth at a time. Spoon into prepared ramekins; sprinkle each serving with 1 teaspoon nuts. Bake at 375° for 20 minutes. Serve immediately. Yield: 4 servings.

CALORIES 221 (37% from fat); FAT 9g (sat 4.8g, mono 3.1g, poly 0.6g); PROTEIN 5.7g; CARB 33.1g; FIBER 1.5g; CHOL 13mg; IRON 1.1mg; SODIUM 174mg; CALC 52mg

When it's time to entertain, don't skip the spectacular dessert. These chocolaty pistachio-crusted soufflés certainly fit the bill. If you're not crazy about pistachios, use your favorite chopped nut instead. Either way, you can't go wrong.

cookies & bars

Lemon-Frosted Sugar Cookies

Using an offset spatula is an easy, mess-free way to frost cookies, bars, and cakes. The metal blade of this spatula is bent near the handle, making the blade lower than the handle. This type of spatula is also useful for removing cookies from baking pans.

Cookies:
    1 cup granulated sugar
    ½ cup butter, softened
    1 large egg
    1 large egg white
    1 tablespoon fat-free milk
    1 teaspoon grated lemon rind
    1 teaspoon vanilla extract
    2 cups all-purpose flour
    ¼ cup toasted wheat germ
    1 teaspoon baking powder
    ½ teaspoon baking soda
    ⅛ teaspoon salt

Frosting:
    2 cups powdered sugar
    1 tablespoon fat-free milk
    1 tablespoon fresh lemon juice
    ¼ teaspoon vanilla extract

Remaining Ingredients:
Food coloring (optional)
Assorted sugar sprinkles (optional)

1. To prepare cookies, beat granulated sugar and butter in a large bowl with a mixer at medium speed until well blended (about 4 minutes). Add egg, egg white, and next 3 ingredients, beating well. Lightly spoon flour into dry measuring cups, and level with a knife. Combine flour and next 4 ingredients in a bowl. Add flour mixture to sugar mixture, stirring well. Spoon dough onto plastic wrap; flatten to a 1½-inch thickness. Cover tightly with plastic wrap; chill 4 hours or overnight.

2. Preheat oven to 400°.

3. Roll dough to a 15 x 12–inch rectangle on a heavily floured surface. Cut dough into 20 (3-inch) squares using a sharp knife. Place squares 2 inches apart on ungreased baking sheets. Bake at 400° for 8 minutes or until golden. Immediately remove cookies from pans using a wide spatula; cool on wire racks.

4. To prepare frosting, combine powdered sugar and next 3 ingredients. Stir in food coloring, if desired. Spread about 2 teaspoons frosting over each cookie with an offset spatula, or place frosting in a small zip-top plastic bag, snip a tiny hole in 1 corner, and drizzle frosting over cookies. Sprinkle with assorted sugar sprinkles, if desired. Yield: 20 cookies (serving size: 1 cookie).

CALORIES 183 (25% from fat); FAT 5.1g (sat 3g, mono 1.3g, poly 0.3g); PROTEIN 2.3g; CARB 32.5g; FIBER 0.7g; CHOL 23mg; IRON 0.8mg; SODIUM 110mg; CALC 21mg

The versatility of these cookies makes them essential for just about any occasion. Lemony and luscious, these refreshing cookies are ideal during spring and summer. Change the color with some food coloring for the perfect Christmas sugar cookie. You may want to start this recipe early in the day, as the dough requires at least four hours to chill.

Peanut Butter Icebox Cookies

1 cup all-purpose flour
¼ teaspoon baking soda
⅛ teaspoon salt
3 tablespoons butter, softened
2 tablespoons chunky peanut
  butter
½ cup packed brown sugar
¼ cup granulated sugar
1 teaspoon vanilla extract
1 large egg white
Cooking spray

1. Lightly spoon flour into a dry measuring cup; level with a knife. Combine flour, baking soda, and salt in a bowl, and set aside.

2. Beat butter and peanut butter with a mixer at medium speed until light and fluffy. Gradually add sugars, beating until well blended. Add vanilla and egg white, and beat well. Add flour mixture; stir well. Turn dough out onto plastic wrap or wax paper, and shape into a 6-inch log. Wrap log in plastic wrap or wax paper, and freeze 3 hours or until firm.

3. Preheat oven to 350°.

4. Cut log into 24 (¼-inch) slices, and place slices 1 inch apart on a baking sheet coated with cooking spray. Bake at 350° for 8 to 10 minutes. Remove cookies from pan, and cool on wire racks. Yield: 2 dozen (serving size: 1 cookie).

CALORIES 66 (29% from fat); FAT 2.1g (sat 1g, mono 0.7g, poly 0.3g); PROTEIN 1g; CARB 10.9g; FIBER 0.3g; CHOL 4mg; IRON 0.4mg; SODIUM 46mg; CALC 6mg

Slice-and-bake cookies are perfect make-ahead treats. Keep logs of dough in your freezer, and then slice and bake the cookies as you need them. Simply turn the dough out onto a surface lined with plastic wrap or wax paper; shape into a 6-inch log. Wrap the plastic wrap or wax paper around the log, twisting the ends tightly to ensure a more cylindrical shape. Freeze until firm, turning the log occasionally to maintain the shape. Use a thin-bladed knife to slice the cookies, and turn the log frequently to prevent flattening on one side.

If you have an affection for cookies and peanut butter, then you can't go wrong with these crisp, crunchy, peanut-buttery gems. If you love peanut butter-and-jelly sandwiches, consider this option: Flatten the log into a shape that resembles toast. Then, after slicing, baking, and cooling, slather a layer of grape or strawberry jelly between two slices of "toast." Kids will especially love this treat.

Gingersnaps

2 cups all-purpose flour
1 tablespoon ground ginger
2 teaspoons baking soda
½ teaspoon salt
1 cup granulated sugar, divided
7 tablespoons butter, softened
¼ cup packed dark brown sugar
2 tablespoons honey
1 teaspoon vanilla extract
1 large egg
Cooking spray

1. Lightly spoon flour into dry measuring cups, and level with a knife. Combine flour and next 3 ingredients in a small bowl. Place ¾ cup granulated sugar, butter, and brown sugar in a large bowl; beat with a mixer at medium speed until well blended. Add honey, vanilla, and egg; beat well. Add flour mixture, beating at low speed until well blended. Cover dough, and freeze 1 hour or until firm.

2. Preheat oven to 350°.

3. Lightly coat hands with cooking spray; shape dough into 24 (1-inch) balls. Roll balls in remaining ¼ cup granulated sugar; place balls 2 inches apart on baking sheets. Bake at 350° for 11 to 12 minutes or until lightly browned. Cool cookies 2 minutes on pans. Remove cookies from pans, and cool on wire racks. Yield: 2 dozen (serving size: 1 cookie).

CALORIES 113 (30% from fat); FAT 3.8g (sat 2.2g, mono 1.1g, poly 0.2g); PROTEIN 1.3g; CARB 18.8g; FIBER 0.3g; CHOL 18mg; IRON 0.5mg; SODIUM 155mg; CALC 5mg

Whether your recipe calls for shaping cookie dough into balls or dropping dough onto a baking pan, a spring-handled cookie scoop makes measuring dough easy. Manufacturers label scoops in different ways. Some are labeled with a number. The higher the number, the smaller the scoop. Be sure to use a scoop that drops the amount of dough called for in the recipe, or the yield will be incorrect. A #70 scoop holds a level table-spoon of dough.

Crispy and flavored like gingerbread, these cookies are precisely what traditional gingersnaps should be. And you'll discover that this homemade version far out-weighs the prepackaged boxed competitors in both flavor and texture. After one bite, you'll never buy commercial brands again.

Coffee-Hazelnut Biscotti

Frangelico is a caramel-colored hazelnut liqueur that's produced in northern Italy. Hints of cacao, vanilla, and coffee combine with toasted hazelnuts to produce the smooth, sweet, and very pleasant liqueur. Legend says that Frangelico was produced in monasteries by the monks. Today, the liqueur is sold in a brown bottle that resembles a monk's habit, including the knotted white cord that is worn around the monk's waist. Frangelico is expensive, but it keeps indefinitely.

2 tablespoons Frangelico (hazelnut-flavored liqueur)
2 tablespoons unsweetened cocoa
1 teaspoon instant espresso or 2 teaspoons instant coffee granules
1 teaspoon vegetable oil
2 large egg whites
1 large egg
1⅓ cups all-purpose flour
½ cup whole wheat flour
½ cup granulated sugar
½ cup packed brown sugar
½ cup coarsely chopped toasted hazelnuts, divided
1 teaspoon baking soda
⅛ teaspoon salt
2 teaspoons ground coffee beans
Cooking spray

1. Preheat oven to 300°.
2. Place liqueur in a small bowl. Microwave at HIGH 10 seconds. Stir in cocoa and espresso until smooth. Add oil, egg whites, and egg, stirring with a whisk until blended.
3. Lightly spoon flours into dry measuring cups; level with a knife. Place flours, sugars, 2 tablespoons hazelnuts, baking soda, and salt in a food processor; process until nuts are ground. Add ground coffee; pulse 2 times or until blended. With processor on, slowly add liqueur mixture through food chute; process until dough forms a ball. Add remaining 6 tablespoons hazelnuts; pulse 5 times or until blended (dough will be sticky). Turn dough out onto a floured surface, and knead lightly 4 or 5 times. Divide into 3 equal portions, shaping each portion into a 10-inch-long roll. Place rolls 3 inches apart on a large baking sheet coated with cooking spray. Bake at 300° for 28 minutes. Remove rolls from pan; cool 10 minutes on a wire rack.
4. Cut each roll diagonally into 20 (½-inch) slices. Place slices, cut sides down, on baking sheets. Bake at 300° for 20 minutes. Turn cookies over; bake an additional 10 minutes (cookies will be soft in center but will harden as they cool). Remove cookies from pans; cool completely on wire racks. Yield: 5 dozen (serving size: 1 biscotto).

CALORIES 38 (24% from fat); FAT 1g (sat 0.1g, mono 0.6g, poly 0.1g); PROTEIN 0.8g; CARB 6.9g; FIBER 0.2g; CHOL 4mg; IRON 0.3mg; SODIUM 30mg; CALC 5mg

A favored pairing with a cup of coffee, biscotti is quite literally a very tough cookie. The biscotti's hardness is due in part to the heaviness of the dough, as well as its two baking times. The dough is formed into loaves that are first baked and then sliced on the diagonal into long pieces. A serrated knife or an electric knife works best in this step, offering a sharp edge to cut through the hard outer surface of the cookie.

Double-Chocolate Cherry Cookies

No matter what they're called—chips, morsels, or chunks—they have one thing in common: They hold their shape and texture during baking. They're perfect for adding to cookies, brownies, muffins, or quick breads. But not all chips are created equal. Chips boasting chocolate liqueur as their first ingredient are sure to have the best flavor. Store chocolate chips tightly wrapped in a cool, dry place. Freezing isn't recommended.

1¼ cups all-purpose flour
½ teaspoon baking powder
¼ teaspoon salt
5 tablespoons butter, softened
½ cup granulated sugar
½ cup packed brown sugar
1½ teaspoons vanilla extract
1 large egg white
⅓ cup dried tart cherries
¼ cup semisweet chocolate chunks
2½ tablespoons premium white chocolate chips
Cooking spray

1. Preheat oven to 350°.

2. Lightly spoon flour into dry measuring cups; level with a knife. Combine flour, baking powder, and salt, stirring with a whisk.

3. Combine butter and sugars in a large bowl; beat with a mixer at medium speed until well blended. Add vanilla and egg white; beat 1 minute. Stir in flour mixture, cherries, chocolate chunks, and chocolate chips.

4. Drop by level tablespoons 2 inches apart onto baking sheets coated with cooking spray. Place pans in freezer 5 minutes. Bake at 350° for 10 minutes or until lightly browned. Cool on pans 2 minutes. Remove cookies from pans; cool completely on wire racks. Yield: 2 dozen (serving size: 1 cookie).

CALORIES 98 (30% from fat); FAT 3.3g (sat 2g, mono 1g, poly 0.1g); PROTEIN 1g; CARB 16.6g; FIBER 0.4g; CHOL 7mg; IRON 0.5mg; SODIUM 63mg; CALC 12mg

We put a tantalizing twist on the traditional chocolate chip cookie by adding dried cherries and premium white chocolate chips. Consider doubling the recipe and sharing with friends and neighbors.

Oatmeal-Raisin Cookies

½ cup granulated sugar
½ cup packed brown sugar
⅓ cup butter, softened
1 teaspoon vanilla extract
⅛ teaspoon salt
1 large egg
1 cup all-purpose flour
1 cup regular oats
½ cup raisins
Cooking spray

1. Preheat oven to 350°.
2. Beat first 6 ingredients with a mixer at medium speed until light and fluffy. Lightly spoon flour into a dry measuring cup, and level with a knife. Add flour and oats to egg mixture, and beat until blended. Stir in raisins. Drop by level tablespoons 2 inches apart onto baking sheets coated with cooking spray. Bake at 350° for 15 minutes or until golden brown. Cool on pans 3 minutes. Remove cookies from pans; cool on wire racks. Yield: 2 dozen (serving size: 1 cookie).

CALORIES 101 (28% from fat); FAT 3.1g (sat 1.7g, mono 0.9g, poly 0.2g); PROTEIN 1.5g; CARB 17.3g; FIBER 0.6g; CHOL 16mg; IRON 0.6mg; SODIUM 43mg; CALC 10mg

Oats contain soluble fiber, which can help lower cholesterol and reduce the risk of heart disease. They are low in fat and contain no sodium or preservatives. They also add a wonderful nutty flavor and a hearty texture to these great cookies. Generally, regular (or "old-fashioned") oats and quick-cooking oats can be used interchangeably in baking, but we usually specify which type to use in our recipes. Instant oats are best avoided because they are preprocessed and too finely cut to add any substance to baked goods.

Fast, simple, and satisfying, oatmeal-raisin cookies are a sure-to-please staple in the American home. They're easy to prepare because they're made with ingredients that you probably have on hand. Your kitchen will smell flavorful and inviting when you pop a batch in the oven.

Easy Lemon Squares

For the best results, bake these bars in an 8-inch square baking pan. Allow the lemon squares to cool completely in the pan on a wire rack before cutting them into bars. This will help ensure a "clean" cut. Finish with a light dusting of powdered sugar shaken through a sieve. Store in an airtight container between layers of wax paper in the refrigerator.

Crust:
- ¼ cup granulated sugar
- 3 tablespoons butter, softened
- 1 cup all-purpose flour

Topping:
- 3 large eggs
- ¾ cup granulated sugar
- 2 teaspoons grated lemon rind
- ⅓ cup fresh lemon juice
- 3 tablespoons all-purpose flour
- ½ teaspoon baking powder
- ⅛ teaspoon salt

Remaining Ingredient:
- 2 teaspoons powdered sugar

1. Preheat oven to 350°.

2. To prepare crust, beat ¼ cup granulated sugar and butter with a mixer at medium speed until creamy. Lightly spoon 1 cup flour into a dry measuring cup; level with a knife. Gradually add 1 cup flour to sugar mixture, beating at low speed until mixture resembles fine crumbs. Press into an 8-inch square baking pan. Bake at 350° for 15 minutes; cool on a wire rack.

3. To prepare topping, beat eggs with a mixer at medium speed until foamy. Add ¾ cup granulated sugar and next 5 ingredients, and beat until blended. Pour over crust. Bake at 350° for 20 minutes. Cool in pan on a wire rack. Sift powdered sugar over top. Yield: 16 servings (serving size: 1 square).

CALORIES 118 (24% from fat); FAT 3.2g (sat 1.7g, mono 1g, poly 0.3g); PROTEIN 2.2g; CARB 20.5g; FIBER 0.3g; CHOL 47mg; IRON 0.6mg; SODIUM 68mg; CALC 16mg

An old-fashioned bar cookie that never goes out of style, our lightened lemon squares taste just like the traditional version. These treats are great with ginger tea on a quiet afternoon or as the luscious finale of a summer cookout.

Butterscotch Bars

½ cup granulated sugar
½ cup packed brown sugar
¼ cup butter, softened
2 large egg whites
1 teaspoon vanilla extract
1¼ cups all-purpose flour
½ teaspoon baking powder
¼ teaspoon salt
Cooking spray
½ cup butterscotch morsels

1. Preheat oven to 350°.

2. Beat sugars and butter with a mixer at medium speed until well blended (about 4 minutes). Add egg whites and vanilla; beat well. Lightly spoon flour into dry measuring cups, and level with a knife. Combine flour, baking powder, and salt; stir well with a whisk. Add flour mixture to sugar mixture; beat at low speed just until blended.

3. Spread batter evenly into an 8-inch square baking pan coated with cooking spray; sprinkle evenly with morsels. Bake at 350° for 25 minutes or until a wooden pick inserted in center comes out clean. Cool in pan on a wire rack. Yield: 16 servings (serving size: 1 bar).

CALORIES 142 (27% from fat); FAT 4.3g (sat 2.6g, mono 1.3g, poly 0.2g); PROTEIN 1.6g; CARB 24g; FIBER 0.3g; CHOL 8mg; IRON 0.6mg; SODIUM 95mg; CALC 24mg

Unlike granulated sugar, which flows freely, brown sugar isn't as refined and contains more moisture. It must be packed into the measuring cup in order to get an accurate measurement. To pack brown sugar, spoon it into a dry measuring cup that is the size the recipe specifies. Press the sugar into the measuring cup with the back of a spoon. Continue to add and pack more sugar until it reaches the rim of the measuring cup. Level with the flat side of a knife, scraping off any excess.

Looking for a tailgate treat, a travel snack, or a lunchbox surprise? If so, these bars are just the ticket. They're every bit as delicious as regular butterscotch brownies, but they have far less fat. With the perfect texture of a crisp crust on top and a moist and soft middle, they disappear fast! They're perfect for your sweet tooth's craving.

cakes

Texas Sheet Cake

When preparing your pan for this recipe, coat the pan with cooking spray before lightly dusting it with flour. Shake the pan to coat the bottom and sides, and shake out excess flour. This method works just as well as the traditional (and more fattening) method of greasing the pan with shortening before flouring.

Cake:
Cooking spray
2 teaspoons all-purpose flour
2 cups all-purpose flour
2 cups granulated sugar
1 teaspoon baking soda
1 teaspoon ground cinnamon
¼ teaspoon salt
¾ cup water
½ cup butter
¼ cup unsweetened cocoa
½ cup low-fat buttermilk
1 teaspoon vanilla extract
2 large eggs

Icing:
6 tablespoons butter
⅓ cup fat-free milk
¼ cup unsweetened cocoa
3 cups powdered sugar
¼ cup chopped pecans, toasted
2 teaspoons vanilla extract

1. Preheat oven to 375°.

2. To prepare cake, coat a 15 x 10–inch jelly-roll pan with cooking spray; dust with 2 teaspoons flour.

3. Lightly spoon 2 cups flour into dry measuring cups; level with a knife. Combine 2 cups flour and next 4 ingredients in a large bowl; stir well with a whisk.

4. Combine water, ½ cup butter, and ¼ cup cocoa in a small saucepan; bring to a boil, stirring frequently. Remove from heat; pour into flour mixture. Beat with a mixer at medium speed until well blended. Add buttermilk, 1 teaspoon vanilla, and eggs; beat well.

5. Pour batter into prepared pan; bake at 375° for 17 minutes or until a wooden pick inserted in center comes out clean. Place pan on a wire rack.

6. To prepare icing, combine 6 tablespoons butter, milk, and ¼ cup cocoa in a medium saucepan; bring to a boil, stirring constantly. Remove from heat; gradually stir in powdered sugar, pecans, and 2 teaspoons vanilla. Spread over hot cake. Cool completely on wire rack. Yield: 20 servings (serving size: 1 slice).

Note: You can also make this recipe in a 13 x 9–inch baking pan. Bake at 375° for 22 minutes.

CALORIES 298 (30% from fat); FAT 10g (sat 5.5g, mono 3.2g, poly 0.7g); PROTEIN 3.1g; CARB 49.8g; FIBER 0.5g; CHOL 44mg; IRON 1.1mg; SODIUM 188mg; CALC 25mg

Why do we love sheet cakes? Well, for starters, they're simple and quick because you don't have to worry about baking cake layers or spreading frosting between the layers. And you can cut the cake into squares and serve it from the pan. Rich in chocolate, this easy charmer boasts a sweet, fudgy icing that would melt in your mouth if not for its pecans.

Gingerbread Squares

1¼ cups all-purpose flour
1 teaspoon ground ginger
1 teaspoon ground cinnamon
½ teaspoon baking soda
½ cup granulated sugar
½ cup low-fat buttermilk
½ cup dark molasses
⅓ cup butter, melted
1 large egg, lightly beaten
Cooking spray
1 tablespoon powdered sugar

1. Preheat oven to 350°.
2. Lightly spoon flour into dry measuring cups; level with a knife. Combine flour, ginger, cinnamon, and baking soda, stirring with a whisk.
3. Combine granulated sugar and next 4 ingredients in a large bowl, stirring with a whisk. Stir in flour mixture. Pour batter into a 9-inch square baking pan coated with cooking spray.
4. Bake at 350° for 25 minutes or until a wooden pick inserted in center comes out clean. Cool in pan on a wire rack. Sprinkle gingerbread with powdered sugar. Yield: 25 servings (serving size: 1 [1¾-inch] square).

CALORIES 84 (30% from fat); FAT 2.8g (sat 1.6g, mono 0.8g, poly 0.2g); PROTEIN 1.1g; CARB 14g; FIBER 0.2g; CHOL 15mg; IRON 0.7mg; SODIUM 61mg; CALC 22mg

The three types of molasses—light, dark, and blackstrap—are the by-products of boiling and refining sugar. The first boiling yields light molasses—a sweet, mild syrup and a great pancake topper. The second boiling produces dark molasses, which we recommend for this recipe. Its rich, not-too-sweet flavor adds moisture and dimension to these gingerbread squares. A third boiling produces blackstrap molasses, which is very dark and thick and has a bitter taste. You may find very old recipes that call for blackstrap molasses, but we do not suggest baking with it.

Surprise your friends with a homemade specialty. These moist squares, which are delicately flavored with ginger, cinnamon, and molasses, are ideal for Christmas or any other time of the year. Simply place these "can't believe they're low-fat" squares in a parchment paper–lined gift box.

Cinnamon-Apple Cake

Thick-skinned, deep red Rome apples are known for their firm flesh and mildly sweet flavor. They're excellent for cooking and baking because their sweet flavor deepens and their texture softens, but they still hold their shape. Try Rome apples in sauces, salads, and pies or other baked goods. Prevent over-ripeness and keep apples fresh by storing them in a sealed plastic bag in the refrigerator for up to six weeks.

1¾ cups sugar, divided
¾ cup (6 ounces) block-style fat-free cream cheese, softened
½ cup butter, softened
1 teaspoon vanilla extract
2 large eggs
1½ cups all-purpose flour
1½ teaspoons baking powder
¼ teaspoon salt
2 teaspoons ground cinnamon
3 cups chopped peeled Rome apple (about 2 large)
Cooking spray

1. Preheat oven to 350°.
2. Beat 1½ cups sugar, cream cheese, butter, and vanilla with a mixer at medium speed until well blended (about 4 minutes). Add eggs, 1 at a time, beating well after each addition; set aside.
3. Lightly spoon flour into dry measuring cups, and level with a knife. Combine flour, baking powder, and salt. Add flour mixture to sugar mixture; beat with a mixer at low speed until blended. Combine remaining ¼ cup sugar and cinnamon. Combine 2 tablespoons of cinnamon mixture and apple in a bowl; stir apple mixture into batter. Pour batter into an 8-inch springform pan coated with cooking spray, and sprinkle with remaining cinnamon mixture.
4. Bake at 350° for 1 hour to 1 hour and 5 minutes or until a wooden pick inserted in center comes out clean. Cool completely in pan on a wire rack. Cut using a serrated knife. Yield: 12 servings (serving size: 1 slice).
Note: You can also make this cake in a 9-inch square cake pan or a 9-inch springform pan; just reduce baking time by 5 minutes.

CALORIES 281 (28% from fat); FAT 8.7g (sat 1.8g, mono 3.7g, poly 2.6g); PROTEIN 4.8g; CARB 46.3g; FIBER 1.2g; CHOL 39mg; IRON 1.1mg; SODIUM 234mg; CALC 89mg

Cinnamon-Apple Cake leads the honor roll of our all-time favorite recipes and is a tasty reminder of what healthy cooking can bring to the table. The cream cheese in the batter gives this cake lots of moisture. Because the cake is so tender, use a serrated knife to cut it.

Pineapple-Coconut-Banana Upside-Down Cake

Upside-down cakes are traditionally made in cast-iron skillets for two reasons. First, cast iron heats more slowly than other materials, preventing the bottom of the cake (which will become the top when serving) from caramelizing too quickly and sticking to the pan. Second, cast iron (unlike other materials) heats evenly, which keeps the cake moist around the edges. Maintaining moisture is important, since this cake isn't frosted and dryness can't be masked.

2 tablespoons butter
¾ cup packed brown sugar
1 (15½-ounce) can pineapple slices in juice, undrained
1 cup flaked sweetened coconut
1 cup all-purpose flour
½ cup granulated sugar
1 teaspoon baking powder
½ teaspoon baking soda
½ teaspoon ground cinnamon
¼ teaspoon salt
½ cup mashed ripe banana (about 1 banana)
2 tablespoons vegetable oil
1 large egg

1. Preheat oven to 375°.

2. Melt butter in a 9-inch cast-iron skillet; sprinkle evenly with brown sugar. Drain pineapple slices over a bowl, reserving ½ cup juice. Place 1 pineapple ring in center of pan. Cut remaining pineapple rings in half, and arrange around center pineapple ring. Sprinkle evenly with coconut. Set aside.

3. Lightly spoon flour into a dry measuring cup, and level with a knife. Combine flour and next 5 ingredients in a large bowl. Combine reserved ½ cup juice, banana, oil, and egg, stirring with a whisk. Add pineapple juice mixture to flour mixture, stirring until combined. Pour flour mixture over coconut. Bake at 375° for 30 minutes or until a wooden pick inserted in center comes out clean. Invert onto a wire rack. Serve warm or at room temperature. Yield: 10 servings (serving size: 1 slice).

CALORIES 301 (27% from fat); FAT 9g (sat 4.9g, mono 1.6g, poly 1.8g); PROTEIN 2.5g; CARB 54.8g; FIBER 1.4g; CHOL 27mg; IRON 1.4mg; SODIUM 231mg; CALC 55mg

This is not your typical upside-down cake—it's even better. Pineapple juice and mashed banana come together in the batter to make a most delicious and delightful dessert that's perfect for special occasions and everyday dining. This cake is excellent both warm and at room temperature.

Blueberry-Blackberry Shortcakes

Measuring flour is the single most important factor in light baking. Baked goods made with less fat tend to dry out, so it's crucial to measure flour accurately. First, fluff the flour with a fork to break up any lumps. Then lightly spoon the flour into a dry measuring cup without compacting it, and level with a knife. Don't scoop the flour out of the canister with the measuring cup because you can get up to 3½ tablespoons per cup too much flour that way. That can make for a very dry shortcake.

Shortcakes:
 2 cups all-purpose flour
 ¼ cup sugar
 1 tablespoon grated lemon rind
 2 teaspoons baking powder
 ½ teaspoon baking soda
 ¼ teaspoon salt
 ¼ cup chilled butter, cut into small pieces
 ½ cup fat-free buttermilk
Cooking spray
 1 teaspoon water
 1 large egg white, lightly beaten
 2 teaspoons sugar

Filling:
 3 cups fresh blueberries, divided
 ½ cup sugar
 2 tablespoons fresh lemon juice
 2 teaspoons cornstarch
 2 cups fresh blackberries

Remaining Ingredients:
 1 cup frozen reduced-calorie whipped topping, thawed
Mint sprigs (optional)

1. Preheat oven to 400°.

2. To prepare shortcakes, lightly spoon flour into dry measuring cups; level with a knife. Combine flour and next 5 ingredients in a large bowl, stirring with a whisk. Cut in chilled butter with a pastry blender or 2 knives until mixture resembles coarse meal. Add buttermilk, and stir just until moist.

3. Turn dough out onto a lightly floured surface; knead lightly 4 times. Pat dough to a ½-inch thickness; cut with a 3-inch biscuit cutter to form 8 dough rounds. Place dough rounds 2 inches apart on a baking sheet coated with cooking spray. Combine water and egg white, stirring with a whisk; brush over dough rounds. Sprinkle evenly with 2 teaspoons sugar. Bake at 400° for 13 minutes or until golden. Remove from oven, and cool on a wire rack.

4. To prepare filling, combine 1 cup blueberries, ½ cup sugar, juice, and cornstarch in a small saucepan. Bring to a boil; reduce heat, and simmer 5 minutes or until slightly thick. Place in a large bowl; add remaining 2 cups blueberries and blackberries, stirring to coat. Cover and chill.

5. Using a serrated knife, cut each shortcake in half horizontally; spoon ½ cup blueberry mixture over bottom half of each shortcake. Top each serving with 2 tablespoons whipped topping and top half of shortcake. Garnish with mint sprig, if desired. Yield: 8 servings (serving size: 1 filled shortcake).

CALORIES 322 (21% from fat); FAT 7.5g (sat 4.7g, mono 1.8g, poly 0.5g); PROTEIN 4.6g; CARB 60.1g; FIBER 4.3g; CHOL 16mg; IRON 1.9mg; SODIUM 354mg; CALC 108mg

During summer, sweet, succulent blueberries and blackberries delight the senses. And they're good for you, too. They're rich in antioxidants, which have been shown to be an important component in the prevention of cancer and heart disease. Let these berries satisfy your sweet tooth as they improve your health.

Old-Fashioned Caramel Layer Cake

When baking a cake, the last thing you want it to do is stick to the pan. For an easy release, coat the pan with cooking spray, line the bottom of the pan with wax paper, coat the paper with cooking spray, and then dust with flour. To ensure that the wax paper fits the pan, trace the bottom of the pan onto the wax paper, and cut out the shape just inside the traced line.

Cake:
Cooking spray
  1 tablespoon all-purpose flour
1½ cups granulated sugar
  ½ cup butter, softened
  2 large eggs
  1 large egg white
2¼ cups all-purpose flour
2½ teaspoons baking powder
  ½ teaspoon salt
1¼ cups fat-free milk
  2 teaspoons vanilla extract

Frosting:
  1 cup packed dark brown
    sugar
  ½ cup evaporated fat-free milk
2½ tablespoons butter
  2 teaspoons light-colored corn
    syrup
Dash of salt
  2 cups powdered sugar
2½ teaspoons vanilla extract

1. Preheat oven to 350°.

2. To prepare cake, coat 2 (9-inch) round cake pans with cooking spray; line bottoms with wax paper. Coat wax paper with cooking spray; dust with 1 tablespoon flour.

3. Beat granulated sugar and ½ cup butter with a mixer at medium speed until well blended (about 5 minutes). Add eggs and egg white, 1 at a time, beating well after each addition. Lightly spoon 2¼ cups flour into dry measuring cups; level with a knife. Combine 2¼ cups flour, baking powder, and salt; stir well with a whisk. Add flour mixture to sugar mixture alternately with 1¼ cups milk, beginning and ending with flour mixture. Stir in 2 teaspoons vanilla.

4. Pour batter into prepared pans; sharply tap pans once on counter to remove air bubbles. Bake at 350° for 25 minutes or until a wooden pick inserted in center comes out clean. Cool in pans 10 minutes on a wire rack, and remove from pans. Peel off wax paper, and cool completely on wire rack.

5. To prepare frosting, combine brown sugar and next 4 ingredients in a saucepan. Bring to a boil over medium-high heat, stirring constantly. Reduce heat; simmer until thick (about 5 minutes), stirring occasionally. Remove from heat. Add powdered sugar and 2½ teaspoons vanilla; beat with a mixer at medium speed until smooth and slightly warm. Cool 2 to 3 minutes (frosting will be thin but will thicken as it cools).

6. Place 1 cake layer on a plate; spread with ½ cup frosting. Top with remaining cake layer. Spread remaining frosting over top and sides of cake. Store cake loosely covered in refrigerator. Yield: 18 servings (serving size: 1 slice).

CALORIES 307 (22% from fat); FAT 7.5g (sat 4.4g, mono 2.2g, poly 0.4g); PROTEIN 3.8g; CARB 56.7g; FIBER 0.4g; CHOL 43mg; IRON 1.2mg; SODIUM 251mg; CALC 97mg

German Chocolate Cake

Overbaking is more of a problem with low-fat cakes than with traditional full-fat versions, and it can result in a dry-textured cake. To prevent it, we suggest testing for doneness about 5 to 10 minutes before the recipe states the cake should finish baking. Test the cake's doneness by inserting a wooden pick into the center of the cake and pulling it straight out. If the wooden pick comes out clean, the cake is done.

Cooking spray
1 tablespoon cake flour
½ cup unsweetened cocoa
1 ounce sweet baking chocolate
½ cup boiling water
1 cup granulated sugar
¾ cup packed brown sugar
3 tablespoons butter, softened
2 tablespoons vegetable oil
¼ cup plain fat-free yogurt
2½ teaspoons vanilla extract
½ teaspoon coconut extract
2 large egg whites
2¼ cups sifted cake flour
2 teaspoons baking powder
½ teaspoon baking soda
½ teaspoon salt
1 cup low-fat or fat-free buttermilk
Coconut-Pecan Frosting (recipe on page 141)

1. Preheat oven to 350°.
2. Coat 3 (8-inch) round cake pans with cooking spray, and dust with 1 tablespoon flour.
3. Combine cocoa and chocolate in a small bowl; add boiling water, stirring until chocolate melts. Set aside.
4. Beat sugars, butter, and oil with a mixer at medium speed until well blended (about 5 minutes). Add yogurt, extracts, and egg whites, beating well after each addition.
5. Combine 2¼ cups flour, baking powder, baking soda, and salt, stirring well with a whisk. Add flour mixture to sugar mixture alternately with buttermilk, beginning and ending with flour mixture. Beat in cocoa mixture.
6. Pour batter into prepared pans; sharply tap pans once on counter to remove air bubbles. Bake at 350° for 25 minutes or until a wooden pick inserted in center comes out clean. Cool in pans 10 minutes on wire racks, and remove from pans. Cool completely on wire racks.
7. Place 1 cake layer on a plate; spread with ⅓ cup Coconut-Pecan Frosting, and top with another cake layer. Spread with ⅓ cup frosting, and top with remaining cake layer. Spread remaining frosting over top and sides of cake. Store cake loosely covered in refrigerator. Yield: 18 servings (serving size: 1 slice).

CALORIES 311 (27% from fat); FAT 9.2g (sat 4.2g, mono 2.6g, poly 1.4g); PROTEIN 4.6g; CARB 52.7g; FIBER 0.3g; CHOL 35mg; IRON 2.2mg; SODIUM 186mg; CALC 111mg

Serving a cake means there's something to celebrate. And with this lightened favorite, there's even more reason to jump for joy. Once you make our German Chocolate Cake, you may never make a full-fat version again. We believe this cake rivals any other German chocolate cake we've ever tasted.

Coconut Triple-Layer Cake with Fluffy Coconut Frosting

To frost, make sure the cake is completely cool. Next, place the first cake layer on a serving platter, and dollop a moderate amount of frosting on the cake's surface. Be sure to use the amount of frosting called for in the recipe for each layer. Otherwise, you may run out of frosting before the cake is completely covered. Spread with a spoon or metal spatula, covering only the top of the layer. Add the next cake layer, and repeat. Add the third cake layer. Spread the remaining frosting over top and sides of the cake, rotating the platter clockwise as you go.

Cooking spray
1 tablespoon cake flour
3½ cups sifted cake flour
2 teaspoons baking powder
¾ teaspoon salt
½ teaspoon baking soda
1¾ cups sugar
¼ cup butter, softened
1½ tablespoons vegetable oil
2 large egg whites
1⅔ cups fat-free milk
½ cup plain fat-free yogurt
2½ teaspoons vanilla extract
¼ teaspoon butter extract
Fluffy Coconut Frosting (recipe on page 141)
¾ cup flaked sweetened coconut, toasted

1. Preheat oven to 350°.
2. Coat 3 (8-inch) round cake pans with cooking spray, and dust with 1 tablespoon flour.
3. Combine 3½ cups flour and next 3 ingredients; stir well with a whisk. Beat sugar, butter, and oil with a mixer at medium speed until well blended (about 5 minutes). Add egg whites, 1 at a time, beating well after each addition. Combine milk and yogurt. Add flour mixture to sugar mixture alternately with milk mixture, beginning and ending with flour mixture. Stir in extracts.
4. Pour batter into prepared pans. Sharply tap pans once on counter to remove air bubbles. Bake at 350° for 25 minutes or until a wooden pick inserted in center comes out clean. Cool in pans 10 minutes on wire racks, and remove from pans. Cool completely on wire racks.
5. Place 1 cake layer on a plate; spread with ⅔ cup Fluffy Coconut Frosting; top with another cake layer. Spread with ⅔ cup frosting, and top with remaining cake layer. Spread remaining frosting over top and sides of cake. Sprinkle coconut around base of cake. Store cake loosely covered in refrigerator. Yield: 16 servings (serving size: 1 slice).

CALORIES 298 (18% from fat); FAT 5.8g (sat 3.3g, mono 1.3g, poly 0.8g); PROTEIN 4.4g; CARB 57.3g; FIBER 0.2g; CHOL 8mg; IRON 2mg; SODIUM 195mg; CALC 83mg

Beautiful and fancy, this is sure to become one of your all-time favorite cake recipes. But there's nothing pretentious about this coconut-flavored layer cake. It's made of three layers of tender, moist cake covered with a smooth and creamy frosting.

Double-Maple Cupcakes

Maple syrup, like honey, is available in different strengths. Lighter syrups are great for adding moisture and an enhanced flavor to your cookies and cakes. For an intense maple flavor in gingerbread and ginger cookies, use darker syrups. Make sure to check the syrup's label before buying it. For the best flavor, buy only brands labeled "pure maple syrup," and refrigerate unused syrup to maintain freshness. Those that are labeled "maple flavored" are actually corn syrups that have been artificially flavored.

Cupcakes:
½ cup granulated sugar
5 tablespoons butter, softened
1 teaspoon vanilla extract
½ teaspoon imitation maple flavoring
2 large eggs
1¼ cups all-purpose flour
1¼ teaspoons baking powder
¼ teaspoon salt
¼ cup 1% low-fat milk
¼ cup maple syrup

Frosting:
3 tablespoons maple syrup
2 tablespoons butter, softened
½ teaspoon vanilla extract
½ teaspoon imitation maple flavoring
⅛ teaspoon salt
1¾ cups sifted powdered sugar

Remaining Ingredient:
12 walnut halves

1. Preheat oven to 350°.
2. To prepare cupcakes, beat first 4 ingredients with a mixer at medium speed until well blended (about 5 minutes). Add eggs, 1 at a time, beating well after each addition. Lightly spoon flour into dry measuring cups; level with a knife. Combine flour, baking powder, and ¼ teaspoon salt in a bowl, stirring well with a whisk. Combine milk and ¼ cup maple syrup. Add flour mixture to sugar mixture alternately with milk mixture, beginning and ending with flour mixture; mix after each addition.
3. Spoon batter into 12 muffin cups lined with paper liners. Bake at 350° for 20 minutes or until a wooden pick inserted in center comes out clean. Cool in pan 10 minutes on a wire rack, and remove from pan. Cool completely on wire rack.
4. To prepare frosting, beat 3 tablespoons maple syrup and next 4 ingredients with a mixer at medium speed 1 minute. Gradually add powdered sugar, beating just until blended (do not overbeat). Spread frosting over cupcakes. Top each cupcake with a walnut half. Yield: 1 dozen (serving size: 1 cupcake).

CALORIES 256 (32% from fat); FAT 9g (sat 4.6g, mono 2.3g, poly 1.4g); PROTEIN 2.9g; CARB 41.5g; FIBER 0.5g; CHOL 53mg; IRON 1mg; SODIUM 186mg; CALC 53mg

These easy cupcakes will bring big smiles to your family and friends. If you'd prefer a cake instead of cupcakes, bake in a 9-inch square baking pan or a 9-inch round cake pan. Spoon the batter into a pan coated with cooking spray. Bake at 350° for 25 minutes until a wooden pick inserted in center comes out clean. Cool in pan; frost top. Serves 12. The nutritional information per serving is the same as for one cupcake.

Triple-Chocolate Cheesecake

We've created breakthrough recipes that rival traditional cheesecakes in richness and texture while cutting the fat in half. One secret is using a combination of fat-free and light cream cheeses. Remove the cheeses from the refrigerator about 30 minutes before making the cheesecake to give them time to soften.

Topping:
    1 tablespoon sugar
    2 teaspoons unsweetened cocoa
    ½ cup reduced-fat sour cream
Crust:
    ⅔ cup chocolate graham cracker crumbs (4 cookie sheets)
    1 tablespoon sugar
    ½ tablespoon butter
    1 tablespoon water
Cooking spray
Filling:
    3 tablespoons dark rum
    3 ounces semisweet chocolate, chopped
    ¼ cup chocolate syrup
    1 (8-ounce) block fat-free cream cheese, softened
    1 (8-ounce) block ⅓-less-fat cream cheese, softened
    1 cup sugar
    2 tablespoons unsweetened cocoa
    ¼ teaspoon salt
    1 teaspoon vanilla extract
    2 large eggs
Remaining Ingredients:
Chocolate shavings (optional)
Fresh raspberries (optional)

1. Preheat oven to 350°.
2. To prepare topping, combine 1 tablespoon sugar and 2 teaspoons cocoa in a small bowl. Add sour cream, stirring until well blended; cover and chill.
3. To prepare crust, combine graham cracker crumbs and 1 tablespoon sugar. Stir in butter and water, blending well. Firmly press mixture into bottom and ½ inch up sides of a 7-inch springform pan coated with cooking spray. Bake at 350° for 8 minutes; remove from oven, and set aside. Reduce oven temperature to 325°.
4. To prepare filling, combine rum and chocolate in a small bowl. Microwave at HIGH 20 seconds; stir until smooth and glossy. Stir in chocolate syrup.
5. Place cheeses in a large bowl; beat with a mixer at low speed until smooth. Combine 1 cup sugar, 2 tablespoons cocoa, and salt; add to cheeses, beating just until smooth. Add rum mixture and vanilla; beat until blended. Add eggs, beating just until blended.
6. Pour cheese mixture into prepared pan, and bake at 325° for 50 minutes or until almost set. Remove cheesecake from oven.
7. Carefully dollop sour cream topping around edges of cheesecake, spreading over top with a small spatula. Return cheesecake to oven.
8. Turn oven off, and cool cheesecake in closed oven 1 hour. Remove cheesecake from oven; run a knife around outside edge. Cool to room temperature. Cover and chill at least 8 hours. Garnish with chocolate shavings and raspberries, if desired. Yield: 12 servings (serving size: 1 wedge).

CALORIES 252 (36% from fat); FAT 10g (sat 6g, mono 1g, poly 0.1g); PROTEIN 7.3g; CARB 33.8g; FIBER 1g; CHOL 55mg; IRON 0.5mg; SODIUM 259mg; CALC 66mg

You won't be able to resist the combination of unsweetened cocoa, chocolate graham cracker crumbs, and semisweet chocolate. Chocolate in the crust, filling, and topping multiplies the joy in this top-rated cheesecake.

pies & pastries

Key Lime Pie

2 large eggs
2 large egg whites
½ cup Key lime juice
1 teaspoon grated lime rind
1 (14-ounce) can fat-free
    sweetened condensed milk
1 (6-ounce) reduced-fat
    graham cracker crust
1½ cups frozen reduced-calorie
    whipped topping, thawed
Lime rind (optional)

1. Preheat oven to 350°.

2. Beat eggs and egg whites with a mixer at medium speed until well blended. Gradually add juice, rind, and milk to egg mixture, beating until well blended. Spoon mixture into crust, and bake at 350° for 20 minutes or until almost set (center will not be firm but will set up as it chills). Cool pie on a wire rack. Cover loosely, and chill 4 hours. Spread whipped topping evenly over filling. Garnish with lime rind, if desired. Yield: 8 servings (serving size: 1 wedge).

CALORIES 288 (18% from fat); FAT 5.9g (sat 3g, mono 1.5g, poly 1.1g); PROTEIN 7.6g; CARB 49.2g; FIBER 0.8g; CHOL 56mg; IRON 0.6mg; SODIUM 198mg; CALC 141mg

Real Key limes are sometimes hard to find, but the bottled juice, which we use in this recipe, is available in most grocery stores. You'll find it alongside the bottled lemon juice. If you're in a pinch, you can substitute lemon juice, but the flavor won't be as tart.

Key lime pie was created by pioneer settlers of the Florida Keys; it's traditionally made with egg yolks, sweetened condensed milk, and lime juice from yellowish green Key limes. Its wonderful not-too-sweet, not-too-tart flavor; creamy texture; and ease of preparation make it one of today's classic recipes. We guarantee that this lightened version will become a family favorite.

Coconut Cream Pie

To make the perfect Italian meringue for this pie, beat the egg whites just until soft peaks form. Overbeating incorporates too much air and will cause the egg whites to separate. Slowly pour the sugar syrup that has cooked to a temperature of 250° into the egg whites, beating with a mixer at high speed until stiff peaks form and the syrup is thoroughly incorporated. The hot sugar syrup heats the egg whites to a safe temperature, so the meringue will be ready to eat after browning only a minute under the broiler.

Crust:
1 (10-inch) Piecrust (recipe on page 139) or ½ (15-ounce) package refrigerated pie dough (such as Pillsbury)

Filling:
¼ cup all-purpose flour
½ cup sugar
⅛ teaspoon salt
2 large eggs
¾ cup 2% reduced-fat milk
¾ cup light coconut milk
¼ teaspoon coconut extract
¼ teaspoon vanilla extract

Meringue:
3 large egg whites
⅔ cup sugar
¼ cup water

Remaining Ingredient:
1 tablespoon flaked sweetened coconut, toasted

1. Prepare and bake Piecrust in a 10-inch deep-dish pie plate. Cool completely on a wire rack.
2. To prepare filling, lightly spoon flour into a dry measuring cup; level with a knife. Combine flour, ½ cup sugar, salt, and eggs in a large bowl; stir well with a whisk.
3. Heat milk and coconut milk over medium-high heat in a small, heavy saucepan to 180° or until tiny bubbles form around edge (do not boil). Gradually add hot milk mixture to sugar mixture, stirring constantly with a whisk. Return milk mixture to pan; cook over medium heat until thick and bubbly (about 10 minutes), stirring constantly.
4. Remove from heat. Spoon custard into a bowl; place bowl in a large ice-filled bowl 10 minutes or until custard comes to room temperature, stirring occasionally. Remove bowl from ice. Stir in extracts; spoon mixture into prepared crust. Cover and chill 8 hours or until firm.
5. Preheat broiler.
6. To prepare meringue, place egg whites in a large bowl; beat with a mixer at high speed until soft peaks form. Combine ⅔ cup sugar and water in a saucepan; bring to a boil. Cook, without stirring, until a candy thermometer registers 250°. Pour hot sugar syrup in a thin stream over egg whites, beating at high speed until stiff peaks form.
7. Spread meringue over chilled pie; sprinkle with coconut. Broil 1 minute or until meringue is lightly browned; cool 5 minutes on a wire rack. Serve immediately. Yield: 10 servings (serving size: 1 wedge).

CALORIES 281 (30% from fat); FAT 9.3g (sat 5.6g, mono 2.6g, poly 0.4g); PROTEIN 5.3g; CARB 45.6g; FIBER 0.6g; CHOL 63mg; IRON 1.4mg; SODIUM 208mg; CALC 28mg

The silky style of coconut cream pie suits a summer table. Though they're simple to make, cream pies need time to chill, sometimes cooling their heels in the fridge for hours on end. Their cold smoothness soothes a parched palate.

Classic Pecan Pie

You can buy pecans in many forms—halves, pieces, and chopped—but whole pecans in the shell are best for freshness and flavor. A good rule of thumb is that 1 pound of unshelled pecans yields about a half a pound of nutmeat (the two edible wrinkled lobes inside the pecan shell), or about 2 cups. Any leftover unshelled pecans can be stored in a cool, dry place for up to six months; shelled pecans may be refrigerated for three months or frozen for six months. Always taste nuts before adding them to a recipe. The fat in nuts can turn rancid, creating a bitter flavor. Rancid nuts will ruin a recipe.

Crust:
   1 cup all-purpose flour
   2 tablespoons granulated sugar
   ½ teaspoon baking powder
   ¼ teaspoon salt
   ¼ cup fat-free milk
   1 tablespoon butter, melted
Cooking spray

Filling:
   1 large egg
   4 large egg whites
   1 cup light-colored or dark corn syrup
   ⅔ cup packed dark brown sugar
   ¼ teaspoon salt
   1 cup pecan halves
   1 teaspoon vanilla extract

1. To prepare crust, lightly spoon 1 cup flour into a dry measuring cup; level with a knife. Combine 1 cup flour, granulated sugar, baking powder, and ¼ teaspoon salt. Add milk and butter; toss with a fork until moist.

2. Press mixture gently into a 4-inch circle on heavy-duty plastic wrap; cover dough with additional plastic wrap. Roll dough, still covered, into an 11-inch circle. Freeze 10 minutes or until plastic wrap can be easily removed.

3. Remove top sheet of plastic wrap; fit dough, plastic wrap side up, into a 9-inch pie plate coated with cooking spray. Remove remaining plastic wrap. Fold edges under, and flute.

4. Preheat oven to 350°.

5. To prepare filling, beat egg, egg whites, and next 3 ingredients with a mixer at medium speed until well blended. Stir in pecan halves and vanilla. Pour mixture into prepared crust. Bake at 350° for 20 minutes; then cover with foil. Bake an additional 23 minutes or until a knife inserted 1 inch from edge comes out clean (do not overbake). Cool on a wire rack. Yield: 10 servings (serving size: 1 wedge).

CALORIES 288 (29% from fat); FAT 9.2g (sat 1.5g, mono 5.1g, poly 2g); PROTEIN 4.3g; CARB 48.1g; FIBER 1g; CHOL 25mg; IRON 1.1mg; SODIUM 253mg; CALC 52mg

No matter how you pronounce it—pih-KAHN, pik-KAN, or even PEE-kan—this pie is 100% delicious. Of the many varieties of nut pies that appear on holiday tables, pecan pie is probably the most popular. We preferred the subtly sweet, crunchy texture of a homemade crust, but you may substitute a crust made from refrigerated pie dough.

Pumpkin Pie

This recipe is a time-saver because it uses refrigerated pie dough instead of dough made from scratch. Pillsbury refrigerated pie dough is the lowest in fat and calories of all the commercial brands we have checked. It's also a little lower in fat and calories than a made-from-scratch piecrust.

Filling:
¾ cup packed brown sugar
1¾ teaspoons pumpkin pie spice
¼ teaspoon salt
1 (12-ounce) can evaporated low-fat milk
2 large egg whites
1 large egg
1 (15-ounce) can unsweetened pumpkin

Crust:
½ (15-ounce) package refrigerated pie dough (such as Pillsbury)
Cooking spray

Topping:
¼ cup whipping cream
1 tablespoon amaretto (almond-flavored liqueur)
2 teaspoons powdered sugar

1. Position oven rack to lowest setting.

2. Preheat oven to 425°.

3. To prepare filling, combine first 6 ingredients in a bowl; stir with a whisk. Add pumpkin, and stir with a whisk until smooth.

4. To prepare crust, roll dough into an 11-inch circle; fit into a 9-inch pie plate coated with cooking spray. Fold edges under, and flute.

5. Pour pumpkin mixture into prepared crust. Place pie plate on a baking sheet. Place pan on lowest oven rack. Bake at 425° for 10 minutes. Reduce oven temperature to 350° (do not remove pie from oven); bake an additional 50 minutes or until almost set. Cool completely on a wire rack.

6. To prepare topping, beat whipping cream with a mixer at high speed until stiff peaks form. Add amaretto and powdered sugar, and beat until blended. Serve with pie. Yield: 12 servings (serving size: 1 pie wedge and about 1 tablespoon topping).

CALORIES 222 (30% from fat); FAT 7.4g (sat 3.7g, mono 0.7g, poly 0.1g); PROTEIN 4.1g; CARB 35.3g; FIBER 3g; CHOL 32mg; IRON 0.8mg; SODIUM 241mg; CALC 104mg

Pies speak to us so clearly of home, of hearth, and of their own indescribable goodness. And a pumpkin pie is no different. A baked single-crust custard pie with a filling of puréed pumpkin, sugar, eggs, milk, and spices, pumpkin pie is traditionally served at Thanksgiving. Refrigerated pie dough makes this recipe simple to prepare. Bake the pie in the lower third of the oven to encourage a crisp crust.

Chocolate Cream Pie

Crust:
 40 graham crackers (10 cookie sheets)
  2 tablespoons sugar
  2 tablespoons butter, melted
  1 large egg white
Cooking spray

Filling:
  2 cups fat-free milk, divided
  ⅔ cup sugar
  ⅓ cup unsweetened cocoa
  3 tablespoons cornstarch
  ⅛ teaspoon salt
  1 large egg
  2 ounces semisweet chocolate, chopped
  1 teaspoon vanilla extract

Remaining Ingredients:
1½ cups frozen reduced-calorie whipped topping, thawed
  ¾ teaspoon grated semisweet chocolate

Our homemade graham cracker crust takes a little more time to prepare than the commercial reduced-fat crust, but the flavor and texture make it worth the effort. Once you have the prepared crumb mixture ready, place about half of the mixture in the bottom of your pie plate after it's been coated with cooking spray. Using both hands, firmly press the crumb mixture against the sides of the pan, rotating the pan until the sides are completely and evenly covered. Place the remaining crumb mixture in the bottom of the pan, spreading it around to cover the pan and firmly pressing down as you go.

1. Preheat oven to 350°.

2. To prepare crust, place crackers in a food processor; process until crumbly. Add 2 tablespoons sugar, butter, and egg white; pulse 6 times or just until moist. Press crumb mixture into a 9-inch pie plate coated with cooking spray. Bake at 350° for 8 minutes; cool on a wire rack 15 minutes.

3. To prepare filling, combine ½ cup milk, ⅔ cup sugar, and next 4 ingredients in a bowl, stirring with a whisk.

4. Heat remaining 1½ cups milk in a small, heavy saucepan over medium-high heat to 180° or until tiny bubbles form around edge (do not boil). Remove from heat. Gradually add hot milk to sugar mixture, stirring constantly with a whisk. Return milk mixture to pan. Add chopped chocolate; cook over medium heat until thick and bubbly (about 5 minutes), stirring constantly. Reduce heat to low, and cook 2 minutes, stirring constantly. Remove from heat, and stir in vanilla. Pour into prepared crust; cover surface of filling with plastic wrap. Chill 3 hours or until firm. Remove plastic wrap; spread whipped topping evenly over filling. Sprinkle with grated chocolate. Yield: 10 servings (serving size: 1 wedge).

CALORIES 242 (30% from fat); FAT 8g (sat 4.6g, mono 2.1g, poly 0.8g); PROTEIN 5g; CARB 38.5g; FIBER 0.1g; CHOL 30mg; IRON 1.4mg; SODIUM 189mg; CALC 83mg

A thick, rich, dark brown layer of decadent chocolate filling is topped with whipped topping and a dusting of grated semisweet chocolate. Simply set it out and watch it go.

Plum Galette

1 cup all-purpose flour
3½ tablespoons chilled butter,
    cut into small pieces
¼ teaspoon salt
3 tablespoons ice water
1 tablespoon cornmeal
4 plums, each cut into 8
    wedges
1 tablespoon cornstarch
¼ cup Plum Jam
1 tablespoon Plum Jam
1 tablespoon sugar

1. Lightly spoon flour into a dry measuring cup, and level with a knife. Combine flour, butter, and salt in a food processor, and process until mixture resembles coarse meal. With processor on, slowly add ice water through food chute, processing just until combined (do not form a ball). Press mixture gently into a 4-inch circle on plastic wrap. Cover and chill 30 minutes.

2. Preheat oven to 425°.

3. Line a baking sheet with parchment paper; sprinkle paper with cornmeal. Unwrap dough; roll dough into a 9-inch circle on a lightly floured surface. Place dough on prepared pan. Combine plums and cornstarch in a large bowl, tossing to coat. Add ¼ cup Plum Jam; toss well to coat. Arrange plum mixture on top of dough, leaving a 1½-inch border. Fold edges of dough over plum mixture. Bake at 425° for 20 minutes.

4. Remove galette from oven (do not turn oven off). Brush crust with 1 tablespoon Plum Jam; sprinkle galette with sugar. Bake at 425° for 20 minutes or until crust is golden brown. Cool on pan 10 minutes on a wire rack before serving. Yield: 6 servings (serving size: 1 wedge).

(Totals include Plum Jam) CALORIES 208 (32% from fat); FAT 7.3g (sat 3.4g, mono 2.8g, poly 0.3g); PROTEIN 2.8g; CARB 33.8g; FIBER 1.6g; CHOL 18mg; IRON 1mg; SODIUM 146mg; CALC 5mg

Plums come in an assortment of colors, from golden-hued to purplish black to bright green. Generally, larger plums are juicier and are best for eating out of hand, while smaller, firmer plums work well in recipes. Refrigerate ripe plums in a plastic bag for three to five days. To ripen hard plums, store them in a paper bag at room temperature for a day or two. Choose tart plums for a less-sweet galette, or select very ripe plums for a sugary result. The jam is a tasty glaze for the galette; serve leftovers spread on toast for breakfast. Refrigerate jam in an airtight container up to three weeks.

Plum Jam

4½ cups chopped ripe red plums
    (about 8 medium)
1 cup sugar
1 cup water

1. Combine all ingredients in a large saucepan; bring to a boil. Cover and reduce heat; simmer 10 minutes. Uncover and simmer 50 minutes or until mixture begins to thicken, skimming foam from surface occasionally. Cool; pour into an airtight container. Cover and chill. Yield: 2 cups (serving size: 2 tablespoons).

CALORIES 68 (4% from fat); FAT 0.3g (sat 0g, mono 0.1g, poly 0.1g); PROTEIN 0.3g; CARB 17.2g; FIBER 0.5g; CHOL 0mg; IRON 0mg; SODIUM 0mg; CALC 0mg

Peach Cobbler

When recipes call for peeled peaches, use a vegetable peeler or a paring knife to peel firm fruit. If working with soft, ripe peaches, blanch them. Cut an "X" into the bottom of each peach, just through the skin. Then bring a large pot of water to a boil and drop in the peaches, cooking them for roughly 20 seconds to 1 minute (the riper the peaches, the quicker they'll cook). Remove the peaches from the water using a slotted spoon, placing them in a sink filled with ice water. Take them out of the water, and use a paring knife or your fingers to remove the skin, which should slide off easily.

2 cups all-purpose flour
1 tablespoon granulated sugar
¼ teaspoon salt
6 tablespoons chilled butter, cut into 6 pieces
6 tablespoons ice water
Cooking spray
6 cups sliced peeled peaches (about 3¾ pounds)
¾ cup packed brown sugar, divided
2½ tablespoons all-purpose flour
1 tablespoon vanilla extract
1 teaspoon ground cinnamon
1 large egg
1 teaspoon water
1 tablespoon granulated sugar

1. Preheat oven to 375°.
2. Lightly spoon 2 cups flour into dry measuring cups; level with a knife. Place flour, 1 tablespoon granulated sugar, and salt in a food processor; pulse 2 or 3 times. Add butter; pulse 10 times or until mixture resembles coarse meal. With processor on, slowly add ice water through food chute, processing just until combined (do not form a ball).
3. Gently press dough into a 4-inch circle. Slightly overlap 2 lengths of plastic wrap on a slightly damp surface. Place dough on plastic wrap; cover with 2 additional lengths of overlapping plastic wrap. Roll dough, still covered, into a 15 x 13–inch rectangle. Place in freezer 5 minutes or until plastic wrap can be easily removed; remove top sheets. Fit dough, plastic wrap side up, into a 2-quart baking dish coated with cooking spray, allowing dough to extend over edges; remove remaining plastic wrap.
4. Combine peaches, ½ cup brown sugar, 2½ tablespoons flour, vanilla, and cinnamon in a large bowl; toss gently. Spoon into prepared dish; fold edges of dough over peach mixture. Sprinkle remaining ¼ cup brown sugar over mixture.
5. Combine egg and 1 teaspoon water in a small bowl. Brush egg mixture over dough; sprinkle with 1 tablespoon granulated sugar. Bake at 375° for 45 minutes or until filling is bubbly and crust is lightly browned. Let stand 30 minutes before serving. Yield: 10 servings.

CALORIES 282 (25% from fat); FAT 7.8g (sat 4.5g, mono 2.1g, poly 0.5g); PROTEIN 4.4g; CARB 49.3g; FIBER 2.4g; CHOL 39mg; IRON 2mg; SODIUM 121mg; CALC 32mg

Cobbler is the premier dessert when peaches are at the apex of ripeness. Brown sugar has an affinity for this luscious seasonal fruit. This cobbler's pastry is especially easy—rather than fussing with the dough to make two separate crusts (top and bottom), just fold the crust over the filling.

Blueberry Crisp à la Mode

6 cups blueberries
2 tablespoons brown sugar
1 tablespoon all-purpose flour
1 tablespoon fresh lemon juice
⅔ cup all-purpose flour
½ cup packed brown sugar
½ cup regular oats
¾ teaspoon ground cinnamon
4½ tablespoons chilled butter,
   cut into small pieces
2 cups vanilla low-fat frozen
   yogurt

1. Preheat oven to 375°.

2. Combine first 4 ingredients in a medium bowl; spoon into an 11 x 7–inch baking dish. Lightly spoon ⅔ cup flour into dry measuring cups, and level with a knife. Combine ⅔ cup flour, ½ cup brown sugar, oats, and cinnamon, and cut in butter with a pastry blender or 2 knives until mixture resembles coarse meal. Sprinkle over blueberry mixture. Bake at 375° for 30 minutes or until bubbly. Top each serving with ¼ cup frozen yogurt. Yield: 8 servings.

Note: The topping may also be made in a food processor. Place ⅔ cup flour, ½ cup brown sugar, oats, and cinnamon in a food processor, and pulse 2 times or until combined. Add butter, and pulse 4 times or until mixture resembles coarse meal.

CALORIES 288 (26% from fat); FAT 8.3g (sat 4.8g, mono 2g, poly 0.9g); PROTEIN 4.2g; CARB 52g; FIBER 3.8g; CHOL 22mg; IRON 1.3mg; SODIUM 96mg; CALC 77mg

Blueberries are an excellent source of disease-fighting antioxidants that may help prevent cancer and heart disease. Low in calories, high in fiber, and virtually fat-free, blueberries are the perfect sweet and healthy summer treat. Although available year-round, buy blueberries when they're in season and are less expensive. Then freeze them to enjoy months later. Look for firm berries with a silvery frost, and discard any that are shriveled and moldy. Don't wash them until you are ready to use them. Store blueberries in the refrigerator for up to five days.

The next time you see a farm stand selling summer-ripe blueberries, make a quick stop. Sample one or two berries to make sure they're juicy and sweet. Then head home to make this comforting dessert. You should have the other ingredients in your pantry. The not-too-sweet flavor comes more from the generous amount of blueberries than from added sugar.

Baklava with Wildflower Honey

As phyllo dough bakes, it becomes wonderfully flaky and crisp. However, it's very delicate and can crack easily. For this recipe, we recommend cutting through the layers of the phyllo with a sharp knife before baking. Afterwards, the honey mixture can seep down through the layers of pastry as the mixture cools. The baklava will be easy to remove from the pan and will display beautifully on a serving plate.

Syrup:
1½ cups wildflower honey
½ cup water
1 tablespoon fresh lemon juice
3 whole cloves
1 (3-inch) cinnamon stick

Filling:
⅔ cup unsalted pistachios, coarsely chopped
½ cup blanched unsalted almonds, coarsely chopped
⅓ cup walnuts, coarsely chopped
¼ cup sugar
¾ teaspoon ground cinnamon
¼ teaspoon ground cardamom
⅛ teaspoon salt

Remaining Ingredients:
Cooking spray
24 (14 x 9–inch) sheets frozen phyllo dough, thawed
1 tablespoon water

1. To prepare syrup, combine first 5 ingredients in a medium saucepan over low heat, and stir until honey is completely dissolved (about 2 minutes). Increase heat to medium; cook, without stirring, until a candy thermometer registers 230° (about 10 minutes). Remove from heat; keep warm. Remove solids with a slotted spoon; discard solids.
2. Preheat oven to 350°.
3. To prepare filling, combine pistachios and next 6 ingredients; set aside.
4. Lightly coat a 13 x 9–inch baking dish with cooking spray. Working with 1 phyllo sheet at a time (cover remaining dough to keep from drying), place phyllo sheet lengthwise in bottom of prepared pan, allowing ends of sheet to extend over edges of dish; lightly coat with cooking spray. Repeat procedure with 5 phyllo sheets and cooking spray for a total of 6 layers. Sprinkle phyllo evenly with one-third of nut mixture (about ⅔ cup). Repeat procedure with phyllo, cooking spray, and nut mixture 2 more times. Top last layer of nut mixture with remaining 6 phyllo sheets, each one lightly coated with cooking spray. Lightly coat top phyllo sheet with cooking spray; press baklava gently into pan. Sprinkle baklava surface with 1 tablespoon water.
5. Make 3 lengthwise cuts and 7 crosswise cuts using a sharp knife to form 32 equal portions. Bake at 350° for 30 minutes or until phyllo is golden brown. Remove from oven. Drizzle honey mixture evenly over baklava. Cool in pan on a wire rack. Store covered at room temperature. Yield: 32 servings (serving size: 1 piece).

CALORIES 117 (27% from fat); FAT 3.5g (sat 0.3g, mono 1g, poly 0.9g); PROTEIN 1.9g; CARB 20.7g; FIBER 0.9g; CHOL 0mg; IRON 0.6mg; SODIUM 53mg; CALC 12mg

Wildflower honey adds a delicate floral scent to this classic dessert, but almond honey would also work well in this recipe. If you can't find unsalted pistachios, use salted pistachios and omit the added ⅛ teaspoon salt.

Apple Turnovers

Phyllo sheets dry out quickly, so be sure to cover the unused sheets with a damp towel. To make the turnovers, work with 1 (4½-inch-wide) strip of dough at a time. Place 2 tablespoons apple mixture at the base of a strip. Fold the right bottom corner over the apple mixture to form a triangle. Continue folding the triangle back and forth to the end of the strip. Place turnover, seam side down, on a baking sheet.

1 large cooking apple, peeled, cored, and quartered
¼ cup chopped dates
2 tablespoons brown sugar
¼ teaspoon salt
4 (14 x 9–inch) sheets frozen phyllo dough, thawed
Butter-flavored cooking spray
¼ cup sifted powdered sugar
½ teaspoon water
⅛ teaspoon vanilla extract

1. Preheat oven to 400°.
2. Place apple in a food processor; pulse 4 times or until apple is finely chopped. Spoon apple into a bowl. Stir in dates, brown sugar, and salt.
3. Place 1 phyllo sheet on a damp towel (cover remaining dough to keep from drying). Lightly coat with cooking spray. Place second phyllo sheet over first sheet; lightly coat with cooking spray. Cut stacked sheets lengthwise into 3 equal strips (each about 4½ inches wide).
4. Working with 1 strip at a time (cover remaining strips), place 2 tablespoons apple mixture at base of strip. Fold the right bottom corner over apple mixture to form a triangle. Continue folding triangle back and forth to end of strip. Place triangle, seam side down, on a baking sheet coated with cooking spray. Repeat Step 4 with remaining 2 phyllo strips. Repeat Steps 3 and 4 with remaining phyllo sheets and apple mixture. Coat triangles with cooking spray.
5. Bake at 400° for 12 minutes or until golden. Remove from pan, and cool 5 minutes on a wire rack.
6. Combine powdered sugar, water, and vanilla, stirring until smooth. Drizzle sugar mixture evenly over turnovers. Serve warm. Yield: 6 turnovers (serving size: 1 turnover).

CALORIES 100 (7% from fat); FAT 0.8g (sat 0.2g, mono 0.4g poly 0.1g); PROTEIN 1.2g; CARB 22.9g; FIBER 1.1g; CHOL 0mg; IRON 0.6mg; SODIUM 159mg; CALC 9mg

A turnover is a round or square piece of pastry dough that's folded over a sweet or savory filling. When folded, the dough forms a semicircle, or, in this case, a triangle. Turnovers can be baked or deep-fried. They can range in size from small to large and can be served as an appetizer, an entrée, or, as we prefer, a dessert. We like the tartness a Granny Smith apple adds to these turnovers, but a Rome or Winesap apple will give you more sweetness.

fruit desserts

Almond-Stuffed Baked Apples with Caramel-Apple Sauce

Stuffed apple halves offer a healthy dessert with a dramatic presentation. To prepare your apples for stuffing, cut them in half. Use a metal measuring spoon or melon baller to scoop out the core and seeds to form a cup that can hold about 1 tablespoon of nut filling. Cut a thin slice off the rounded side of each apple half so it will sit flat on the baking pan.

Filling:
- ½ cup sliced almonds, toasted
- ¼ cup sugar
- 2 teaspoons butter, melted
- ¼ teaspoon vanilla extract
- ⅛ teaspoon salt
- Dash of ground nutmeg
- 1 large egg white, lightly beaten

Apples:
- 4 Braeburn apples, halved
- Cooking spray
- 1 tablespoon sugar
- ¼ teaspoon ground cinnamon

Sauce:
- ½ cup sugar
- 3 tablespoons water
- ½ cup apple cider
- 1 tablespoon brandy
- 1 tablespoon Grand Marnier (orange-flavored liqueur)
- 1 teaspoon butter
- Dash of salt

1. Preheat oven to 350°.

2. To prepare filling, place almonds in a food processor; process until finely ground. Combine ground almonds, ¼ cup sugar, and next 5 ingredients, stirring until well combined.

3. To prepare apples, core carefully, scooping out 1 tablespoon from each apple half to form a cup. Cut a thin slice off rounded side of each apple half so it will sit flat. Place apples, cup sides up, on a jelly-roll pan coated with cooking spray. Combine 1 tablespoon sugar and cinnamon; sprinkle generously over apples. Spoon about 1 tablespoon filling in cup of each apple half. Bake at 350° for 40 minutes or until apples are golden and tender.

4. To prepare sauce, combine ½ cup sugar and 3 tablespoons water in a small saucepan. Cook over medium-high heat until mixture begins to brown (do not stir); gently tilt pan, and swirl to evenly brown mixture. Reduce heat to low; slowly add cider, stirring constantly. Remove from heat; stir in brandy and next 3 ingredients. Serve over apples. Yield: 8 servings (serving size: 1 stuffed apple half and 1½ tablespoons sauce).

CALORIES 185 (22% from fat); FAT 4.5g (sat 1.1g, mono 2.3g, poly 0.8g); PROTEIN 1.7g; CARB 34.4g; FIBER 3.1g; CHOL 4mg; IRON 0.2mg; SODIUM 78mg; CALC 18mg

These stuffed apples come together in minutes and bake while you enjoy dinner. When you caramelize the sugar, don't stir or move the pan until the sugar melts and begins to brown. The caramel mixture will splatter when you add the cider, so use a long-handled wooden spoon for stirring.

Poached Pears

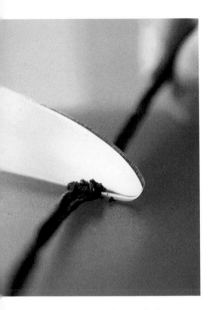

Cooking with vanilla beans instead of the commercial extract adds a profound flavor to many dishes. The difference is well worth the effort. Most supermarkets carry vanilla beans in the spice section. Extracting the pulp from the pod is simple. Using a small knife with a pointed tip, cut the vanilla bean in half lengthwise. Scrape out the seeds with the knife blade, or push them out of the vanilla half with your thumbnail.

4 large Bosc pears
1 cup water
1 cup dry white wine
2 tablespoons sugar
2 tablespoons honey
4 dried apricots
2 (3 x ½–inch) lemon rind strips
1 (3-inch) piece vanilla bean, split lengthwise, or 1 teaspoon vanilla extract
1 whole clove
4 reduced-fat vanilla wafers, crushed
5 tablespoons coarsely chopped pistachios, toasted and divided

1. Peel pears. Cut each pear in half, and core, leaving stems intact. Slice about ¼ inch from base of each pear so it will sit flat.

2. Combine water and next 7 ingredients in a large saucepan; bring to a boil. Add pears; cover, reduce heat, and simmer 10 minutes or until tender. Remove pears and apricots from cooking liquid using a slotted spoon; chill pears and apricots. Bring cooking liquid to a boil; cook until reduced to 1 cup (about 15 minutes). Strain cooking liquid through a sieve over a bowl; discard solids. Chill.

3. Chop apricots. Combine apricots, wafer crumbs, and 1 tablespoon pistachios. Place 2 pear halves in each of 4 bowls. Spoon about 1 tablespoon apricot mixture into each pear cavity. Spoon ¼ cup syrup over each pear; sprinkle each with 1 tablespoon pistachios. Yield: 4 servings.

Note: Use a melon baller to core pears.

CALORIES 251 (22% from fat); FAT 6g (sat 0.7g, mono 3.4g, poly 0.9g); PROTEIN 3.4g; CARB 51.5g; FIBER 6g; CHOL 0mg; IRON 1.7mg; SODIUM 24mg; CALC 41mg

Don't be deceived. As elegant and classy as they appear, poached pears are easy to prepare. Sweet-tart Bosc pears and dried apricots simmer in a fragrant mixture of wine, honey, cloves, and vanilla.

Brennan's Bananas Foster

4 medium bananas
¼ cup butter
1 cup packed brown sugar
¼ cup crème de banane
   (banana liqueur)
½ teaspoon ground cinnamon
¼ cup dark rum
2 cups vanilla low-fat ice
   cream

1. Peel bananas; cut each banana in half lengthwise. Cut each half crosswise into 2 pieces.

2. Melt butter in a large nonstick skillet over medium heat. Stir in brown sugar, liqueur, and cinnamon. Bring to a simmer, and cook 2 minutes. Add bananas; cook 4 minutes or until tender. Remove from heat. Add rum to pan, and ignite rum with a long match. Stir bananas gently until flame dies down. Serve over ice cream. Yield: 8 servings (serving size: ¼ cup ice cream, 2 banana pieces, and 2 tablespoons sauce).

CALORIES 290 (21% from fat); FAT 6.9g (sat 3.4g, mono 2.4g, poly 0.3g); PROTEIN 2.2g; CARB 51.4g; FIBER 2.1g; CHOL 18mg; IRON 0.7mg; SODIUM 74mg; CALC 79mg

The "flambé" cooking technique is the important final step in making bananas Foster. The alcohol is set aflame and allowed to burn off, leaving a more intense flavor. To flambé, remove the skillet from the heated cooktop, and add rum. For safety, ignite the rum using a long match. The flames will die out naturally as you stir the bananas, creating a delicious syrup that coats the fruit.

Bananas Foster is an exquisite dessert made of sliced bananas that are first sautéed in butter and sugar and then flambéed in rum and spooned over ice cream. First made in the 1950s in New Orleans at Brennan's Restaurant, the Brennan family named the recipe after Richard Foster, one of their favorite customers. Even today it's one of their most requested desserts.

Cherries in Spiced Wine Syrup with Pound Cake Croutons

Cherries open the stone-fruit season in late May. Dark red Bing cherries are the popular American standard. Cherries do not ripen after the harvest, so once picked, their sweetness is set. Here's a good rule of thumb: The darker the cherry, the sweeter it is. Store fresh cherries for up to a week in the refrigerator in a bowl lined with paper towels.

½ teaspoon grated lemon rind
6 black peppercorns
1 (3-inch) cinnamon stick
1 (4-inch) rosemary sprig
2 cups dry red wine
¾ cup brandy
½ cup water
⅓ cup honey
2 tablespoons fresh lemon juice
3 cups pitted sweet cherries
½ (10.75-ounce) loaf frozen low-fat pound cake (such as Sara Lee)
Cooking spray
⅓ cup reduced-fat sour cream
1 tablespoon honey

1. Place first 4 ingredients on a double layer of cheesecloth. Gather edges of cheesecloth together; tie securely.
2. Combine wine and next 4 ingredients in a medium saucepan; bring to a boil. Add cheesecloth bag, and cook 5 minutes. Reduce heat, and add cherries; simmer 5 minutes, stirring occasionally. Drain cherries in a colander over a bowl, reserving cooking liquid.
3. Place cherries in a medium bowl; discard cheesecloth bag. Return cooking liquid to pan; bring to a boil. Cook 20 minutes or until reduced to 1¼ cups. Pour wine syrup over cherries, and refrigerate 1½ hours or until mixture is completely cool.
4. Preheat oven to 350°.
5. Cut cake into 24 (1-inch) cubes, and arrange cake cubes in a single layer on a nonstick baking sheet coated with cooking spray. Bake at 350° for 12 minutes or until lightly browned, turning cubes every 4 minutes.
6. Combine sour cream and 1 tablespoon honey. Spoon ½ cup cherry mixture into each of 6 bowls or parfait glasses; top each serving with 4 croutons and 1 tablespoon sour cream mixture. Yield: 6 servings.

CALORIES 283 (20% from fat); FAT 6.4g (sat 2.4g, mono 1.9g, poly 0.5g); PROTEIN 3.1g; CARB 48.5g; FIBER 1.7g; CHOL 31mg; IRON 1.3mg; SODIUM 146mg; CALC 48mg

Capture the flavor of early summer by serving Cherries in Spiced Wine Syrup. Rosemary, cinnamon, and peppercorns give the red-wine sauce a robust flavor. We served the cherry mixture with toasted pound cake, but it's equally good served over vanilla ice cream.

Stuffed Figs with Marsala

1 cup sweet Marsala
¼ cup orange juice
2 tablespoons sugar
12 dried Calimyrna figs
⅓ cup (3 ounces) ⅓-less-fat
cream cheese, softened
¼ cup (1 ounce) grated fresh
Parmesan cheese
1 tablespoon chopped pine
nuts
Orange rind curls (optional)
Mint sprigs (optional)
Pine nuts (optional)

1. Combine first 4 ingredients in a small saucepan; bring to a boil. Remove from heat; cover and let stand 15 minutes. Remove figs from pan with a slotted spoon; set aside, and keep warm. Bring Marsala mixture to a boil; cook 10 minutes or until reduced to ¼ cup.

2. Combine cheeses and chopped pine nuts in a small bowl; stir until well blended. Cut each fig to, but not through, stem end. Stuff about 1½ teaspoons cheese mixture into center of each fig. Spoon 1 tablespoon Marsala sauce onto each of 4 dessert plates; arrange 3 stuffed figs on top of sauce. Garnish with orange rind curls, mint sprigs, and pine nuts, if desired. Yield: 4 servings.

CALORIES 288 (28% from fat); FAT 9.1g (sat 4.4g, mono 2.8g, poly 1.4g); PROTEIN 6.3g; CARB 50.1g; FIBER 7.1g; CHOL 20mg; IRON 1.6mg; SODIUM 179mg; CALC 163mg

Since this recipe begins with dried figs, they must first be hydrated in Marsala and orange juice so the figs will become plump and tender. To prepare the figs for stuffing, snip each fig to, but not through, the stem end in an "X" pattern with a pair of kitchen shears. Gently spread open each cut fig to allow room for the cream cheese filling. For a perfect presentation, use a small melon baller or a small cookie dough scoop to spoon the filling into the center of each fig.

Fresh figs are extremely perishable and are available only twice a year: from June through July and from September through October. We opted to use dried figs in this recipe so that you could enjoy it year-round.

Strawberries and Oranges with Vanilla-Scented Wine

To section an orange, begin by peeling the fruit with a paring knife, being sure to remove the white pith, which can be bitter. Next, hold the peeled orange over a bowl, and slice between the membranes. Lift the segment out with the knife blade. The bowl will catch the juices.

1 cup late-harvest riesling or other dessert wine
3 (4-inch) orange rind strips
½ cup fresh orange juice
1 tablespoon sugar
1 (3-inch) piece vanilla bean, split lengthwise
3 cups halved strawberries
1¼ cups orange sections
Mint sprigs (optional)

1. Combine first 4 ingredients in a medium saucepan. Scrape seeds from vanilla bean; add seeds and bean to wine mixture. Bring to a boil; reduce heat, and simmer 5 minutes. Strain mixture through a sieve over a large bowl; discard solids. Let cool 30 minutes. Stir in strawberries and orange sections. Cover and chill. Garnish with mint sprigs, if desired. Yield: 6 servings (serving size: ⅔ cup).

CALORIES 60 (6% from fat); FAT 0.4g (sat 0g, mono 0.1g, poly 0.2g); PROTEIN 1g; CARB 14.5g; FIBER 2.7g; CHOL 0mg; IRON 0.5mg; SODIUM 4mg; CALC 31mg

Late-harvest riesling is sweeter than other rieslings. If you can't find it, try an equally sweet dessert wine, such as Sauternes, Muscat, or late-harvest Gewürztraminer. Prepare and chill this refreshingly light dessert early in the day. For a nonalcoholic version, use white grape juice in place of the wine.

Tropical-Fruit Sundaes

1 cup chopped kiwifruit
(about 2)
1 cup chopped mango (about
1 medium)
3 tablespoons orange juice
1 tablespoon lime juice
2 cups pineapple sherbet
4 teaspoons flaked sweetened
coconut, toasted

1. Combine first 4 ingredients in a small bowl; cover and chill 30 minutes. Spoon ½ cup sherbet into each of 4 dessert dishes. Top sherbet evenly with fruit mixture, and sprinkle with coconut. Serve immediately. Yield: 4 servings (serving size: ½ cup sherbet, ½ cup fruit, and 1 teaspoon coconut).

CALORIES 174 (12% from fat); FAT 2.4g (sat 1.4g, mono 0.5g, poly 0.2g); PROTEIN 1.7g; CARB 38.2g; FIBER 4.6g; CHOL 0mg; IRON 0.4mg; SODIUM 37mg; CALC 61mg

A mango can be tricky to cut because it has a rather large seed that grows inside the fruit. To remove the flesh from a mango, begin by holding the fruit, stem end up, on a cutting board. With a sharp knife, slice the fruit lengthwise down each side of the flat pit. Holding a mango half in the palm of your hand, score the pulp in square cross-sections. Be sure that you slice to, but not through, the skin. Finally, turn the mango inside out, and cut the chunks from the skin. Chop to the desired size.

Some of the best desserts from around the globe come from nature in the form of sweet, juicy fruit. Tropical fruit in particular is sure to get your taste buds excited. Kiwi, mango, orange, lime, and pineapple flavors receive well-deserved attention in this fruit-filled sundae.

Blueberry Gelato

2 cups fresh or frozen
  blueberries
¼ cup blueberry preserves
¼ cup water
¼ teaspoon salt
⅔ cup sugar
3 large egg yolks
2 cups 2% reduced-fat milk
2 tablespoons fresh lemon
  juice
Fresh blueberries (optional)

When combining eggs and a hot liquid, such as milk, it's important to acclimate the eggs to the temperature of the hot liquid in stages so they don't curdle. To "temper" your egg mixture, whisk one-third of the hot milk into the egg mixture in a slow, steady stream. Then whisk your egg-and-milk mixture back into the pan of hot milk, and cook as directed. When it's done, the custard should coat a spoon and be thick enough so that when you run a finger across the back of the spoon, the mark remains. If egg particles show, the custard is overcooked.

1. Combine first 4 ingredients in a medium nonaluminum saucepan, and bring to a boil. Reduce heat to medium; cook 10 minutes. Place mixture in a blender, and process until smooth.

2. Beat sugar and egg yolks in a large bowl with a whisk until thick and pale (about 5 minutes). Heat milk over medium-high heat in a small, heavy saucepan to 180° or until tiny bubbles form around edge of pan, stirring frequently (do not boil). Add one-third hot milk mixture to egg mixture, stirring with a whisk. Gradually add to remaining hot milk mixture, stirring constantly with a whisk. Cook over medium-low heat until mixture coats back of a spoon (about 4 minutes). Remove from heat. Stir in blueberry mixture, and cool completely. Stir in juice.

3. Pour mixture into the freezer can of an ice-cream freezer, and freeze according to manufacturer's instructions. Garnish with blueberries, if desired. Yield: 3 cups (serving size: ½ cup).

CALORIES 213 (22% from fat); FAT 4.4g (sat 1.8g, mono 1.5g, poly 0.5g); PROTEIN 4.5g; CARB 38.4g; FIBER 1.3g; CHOL 115mg; IRON 0.5mg; SODIUM 145mg; CALC 114mg

The first sweet taste will show you why Italians are so passionate about gelato. Gelato, which comes from gelare, the Italian word meaning "to freeze," is the umbrella term for any frozen Italian dessert. But in addition to its general definition, it also refers to a milk-based concoction with a dense, buttery consistency similar to that of American ice cream. You can serve it in a cup or in an ice-cream cone. Blueberries give this frozen treat a vibrant color. For the best results and flavor, cook the blueberry mixture in a nonaluminum pan.

Lemon-Ginger Sorbetto

Ginger has a refreshing flavor that complements many desserts, but the root's fibrous texture isn't exactly ideal for a smooth sorbetto. In this recipe, we used ginger juice instead. To extract the juice, place grated ginger on several layers of damp cheesecloth. Gather the ends of the cheesecloth together, forming a tight pocket of ginger at the base. Squeeze the ginger through the cheesecloth over a bowl to catch the juice. Discard the cheesecloth.

3 cups water
1 cup sugar
6 tablespoons honey
1 (2-inch) piece peeled fresh ginger
1 cup fresh lemon juice (about 8 lemons)
Lemon slices (optional)

1. Combine water and sugar in a large saucepan, and bring to a boil, stirring until sugar dissolves. Remove from heat, and stir in honey. Cool completely.

2. Grate ginger; place ginger on several layers of damp cheesecloth. Gather edges of cheesecloth; squeeze cheesecloth bag over a small bowl to measure 1 tablespoon ginger juice. Combine sugar mixture, ginger juice, and lemon juice in a large bowl.

3. Pour mixture into the freezer can of an ice-cream freezer, and freeze according to manufacturer's instructions. Spoon sorbetto into a freezer-safe container; cover and freeze 1 hour or until firm. Garnish with lemon slices, if desired. Yield: 4 cups (serving size: ½ cup).

CALORIES 153 (0% from fat); FAT 0g; PROTEIN 0.2g; CARB 40.7g; FIBER 0.1g; CHOL 0mg; IRON 0.1mg; SODIUM 1mg; CALC 4mg

Live la dolce vita *with a sweet, cold spoonful of* sorbetto. *Sorbetto is a fruit-based gelato that contains no dairy products and is best known as sorbet. Whip up this icy treat on any summer night, and you won't need a trip to Italy's Arno River or the Grand Canal to make memories.*

custards, puddings & soufflés

Vanilla Bean Crème Brûlée

A water bath (a shallow pan of hot water in which containers of food are cooked) insulates and protects custards from the heat of the oven so they cook slowly and evenly. The depth of the water should be half the height of the custard container (ramekin, cake pan, etc.). It's a good idea to cover the bottom of the pan with a dish towel to prevent the custards from coming into direct contact with the hot pan. If you're baking multiple custards, the pan must be large enough so that the containers don't touch.

4 large egg yolks
1 teaspoon granulated sugar
⅛ teaspoon salt
2 cups 2% reduced-fat milk
1 (3-inch) piece vanilla bean, split lengthwise, or 1 teaspoon vanilla extract
3 tablespoons granulated sugar
¾ cup nonfat dry milk
¼ cup packed light brown sugar
1½ teaspoons water

1. Preheat oven to 300°.
2. Combine first 3 ingredients in a medium bowl; stir well with a whisk. Set aside.
3. Pour reduced-fat milk into a medium saucepan. Scrape seeds from vanilla bean; add seeds, bean, 3 tablespoons granulated sugar, and dry milk to pan. Heat mixture over medium heat to 180° or until tiny bubbles form around edge (do not boil), stirring occasionally with a whisk. Discard bean.
4. Gradually add hot milk mixture to egg mixture, stirring constantly with a whisk. Divide milk mixture evenly among 6 (4-ounce) ramekins or custard cups. Place ramekins in a 13 x 9–inch baking pan; add hot water to pan to a depth of 1 inch. Bake at 300° for 1 hour or until center barely moves when ramekin is touched. Remove ramekins from pan; cool completely on a wire rack. Cover and chill at least 4 hours or overnight.
5. Combine brown sugar and 1½ teaspoons water in a 1-cup glass measure. Microwave at HIGH 30 seconds, and stir until sugar dissolves. Microwave at HIGH 60 seconds; pour evenly over desserts, quickly tipping ramekins to coat tops of brûlées (there will be a thin layer of melted sugar). Let harden. Yield: 6 servings (serving size: 1 custard).

CALORIES 185 (25% from fat); FAT 5.2g (sat 2.1g, mono 1.8g, poly 0.5g); PROTEIN 10g; CARB 24.7g; FIBER 0g; CHOL 155mg; IRON 0.6mg; SODIUM 177mg; CALC 309mg

Literally, crème brûlée *means "burnt cream." This dessert is a baked and chilled custard that has a crunchy sugar-coated topping. The sugar is quickly caramelized, forming a brittle topping that is a delicious contrast to the creamy custard.*

Cuban Coconut Rice Pudding

3 cups water
1 cup short-grain rice (such as Arborio or Valencia)
4 whole cloves
1 (2-inch) piece vanilla bean, split lengthwise
1 (2-inch) cinnamon stick
1 (14-ounce) can fat-free sweetened condensed milk
½ cup evaporated fat-free milk
½ cup light coconut milk
½ cup golden raisins
1 tablespoon chopped crystallized ginger
1 teaspoon grated lemon rind
Pinch of salt

1. Place water and rice in a large saucepan. Place cloves, vanilla, and cinnamon stick on a double layer of cheesecloth. Gather edges of cheesecloth together; tie securely. Add to rice mixture. Bring to a simmer over medium heat, stirring frequently. Reduce heat to low; cook 20 minutes or until rice is tender and liquid is almost absorbed.

2. Stir in milks and raisins, and cook 10 minutes, stirring frequently. Stir in ginger, lemon rind, and salt; cook 5 minutes, stirring frequently. Remove cheesecloth with spices; discard. Pour rice mixture into a bowl or individual bowls; cover surface of rice mixture with plastic wrap. Chill. Yield: 8 servings (serving size: ½ cup).

CALORIES 286 (3% from fat); FAT 1g (sat 0.7g, mono 0.1g, poly 0.1g); PROTEIN 7g; CARB 61.9g; FIBER 0.8g; CHOL 7mg; IRON 1.7mg; SODIUM 95mg; CALC 184mg

Any starchy short-grain rice, such as Arborio, Valencia, or Japanese white rice, works well in this creamy pudding. As the rice cooks, the starch on the outer surface of the grain softens and dissolves into the water and milk. As the pudding is stirred and continues to cook, the starch thickens the liquid, coating the grains of rice with a rich, creamy, sweet sauce.

This Cuban-inspired pudding is the quintessential comfort food. It uses starchy Arborio rice, which produces a creaminess reminiscent of risotto. The coconut milk enhances the spicy flavor and contributes extra richness.

Vanilla-Nut Pudding

6 tablespoons sugar
2 tablespoons cornstarch
2 cups 1% low-fat milk, divided
⅛ teaspoon salt
1 large egg, lightly beaten
1 teaspoon vanilla extract
2 tablespoons finely chopped
  pistachios, toasted
1 tablespoon finely chopped
  blanched almonds, toasted
Grated whole nutmeg (optional)

1. Combine sugar and cornstarch in a medium heavy saucepan. Add ½ cup milk; stir with a whisk until well blended. Add remaining 1½ cups milk and salt; bring to a simmer over medium heat, stirring frequently. Reduce heat to medium-low; cook 9 minutes, stirring frequently.

2. Place egg in a medium bowl. Gradually add hot milk mixture, stirring constantly with a whisk. Place egg mixture in pan; cook over medium-low heat 3 minutes or until thick, stirring constantly. Remove from heat; stir in vanilla. Pour into individual bowls; cover surface of pudding with plastic wrap. Cool completely. Uncover and sprinkle with nuts. Garnish with nutmeg, if desired. Yield: 4 servings (serving size: ½ cup).

CALORIES 197 (25% from fat); FAT 5.4g (sat 1.5g, mono 2.4g, poly 1g); PROTEIN 6.9g; CARB 30.1g; FIBER 0.7g; CHOL 58mg; IRON 0.5mg; SODIUM 151mg; CALC 166mg

When lightly dispensed, salt can enhance the flavor of many foods so that they don't taste flat. In fact, pastry chefs always advise adding a pinch of salt to desserts. Salt suppresses any bitter notes and brings out sweetness. Think of salt as a supporting player—one that lets the taste of other ingredients shine and creates harmony among all the components in a dish.

It doesn't take much longer to make this pudding than it does to make a "cook and serve" pudding from a box, and the silky, smooth texture and rich vanilla flavor will convince you that it's worth the effort. We liked the crunch of the toasted nuts, but you can serve it with fresh strawberries, peaches, or blueberries, too.

Mocha Pudding

⅓ cup sugar
2 tablespoons cornstarch
1 tablespoon instant coffee
   granules
⅛ teaspoon salt
2 cups 1% low-fat milk
¼ cup semisweet chocolate
   minichips
1 large egg yolk, beaten
1 teaspoon vanilla extract
Whipped topping (optional)
Grated chocolate (optional)

1. Combine first 4 ingredients in a medium saucepan. Gradually add milk, stirring with a whisk until blended.
2. Stir in chocolate. Cook over medium heat 7 minutes or until mixture comes to a boil, stirring constantly. Reduce heat, and simmer 1 minute, stirring constantly.
3. Gradually stir about one-fourth of hot mixture into egg yolk; add to remaining hot mixture. Cook 2 minutes, stirring constantly. Remove from heat; stir in vanilla. Pour into individual glasses; cover pudding with plastic wrap, gently pressing plastic directly onto pudding. Chill until set. Garnish with whipped topping and grated chocolate, if desired. Yield: 4 servings (serving size: ½ cup).

CALORIES 202 (25% from fat); FAT 5.6g (sat 3.1g, mono 1.9g, poly 0.3g); PROTEIN 5.3g; CARB 33.8g; FIBER 0.7g; CHOL 56mg; IRON 0.6mg; SODIUM 138mg; CALC 161mg

Instant coffee granules have found a place in today's pantry that extends beyond a quick morning cup of hot coffee. Instead, you'll find instant coffee granules and instant espresso powder used as flavorful ingredients in both savory and sweet dishes. Here, instant coffee granules dissolve in the hot milk, adding rich depth of flavor to the chocolate pudding.

Humble in appearance and honest in flavor, chocolate pudding makes a simple, satisfying weeknight dessert. Add a little coffee, and the balance of flavors shifts from basic to intriguing. Spoon the pudding into your prettiest stemmed glasses, add a dollop of whipped topping, and sprinkle with grated chocolate. You'll have an elegant, grown-up dessert.

Blackberry-Lemon Pudding Cake

Research shows that black-berries contain anthocyanins, which are antioxidants that help produce insulin, lower blood sugar levels, and reduce the risk of develop-ing some forms of cancer. The berries are purplish black and range in size from ½ inch to 1 inch long. They're usually available from May through August. Buy plump berries with a deep color and without hulls or stems. If the hulls are still attached, the berries are not mature and will be tart.

¼ cup all-purpose flour
⅔ cup granulated sugar
⅛ teaspoon salt
⅛ teaspoon ground nutmeg
1 cup low-fat buttermilk
1 teaspoon grated lemon rind
¼ cup fresh lemon juice
2 tablespoons butter, melted
2 large egg yolks
3 large egg whites
¼ cup granulated sugar
1½ cups blackberries
Cooking spray
¾ teaspoon powdered sugar

1. Preheat oven to 350°.
2. Lightly spoon flour into a dry measuring cup, and level with a knife. Combine flour, ⅔ cup granulated sugar, salt, and nutmeg in a large bowl; add buttermilk, lemon rind, and next 3 ingredients, stirring with a whisk until mixture is smooth.
3. Beat egg whites with a mixer at high speed until foamy. Add ¼ cup granulated sugar, 1 tablespoon at a time, beat-ing until stiff peaks form. Gently stir one-fourth of egg white mixture into buttermilk mixture; gently fold in remaining egg white mixture. Fold in blackberries.
4. Pour batter into an 8-inch square baking pan coated with cooking spray. Place in a larger baking pan, and add hot water to larger pan to a depth of 1 inch. Bake at 350° for 35 minutes or until cake springs back when touched lightly in center. Sprinkle cake with powdered sugar. Serve warm. Yield: 5 servings (serving size: 1 cup).

CALORIES 285 (23% from fat); FAT 7.2g (sat 1.7g, mono 2.8g, poly 1.8g); PROTEIN 6g; CARB 51.2g; FIBER 3.3g; CHOL 89mg; IRON 0.8mg; SODIUM 198mg; CALC 86mg

As spring transitions into summer, you're most likely craving a dessert that's not too heavy. This treat is not quite a pudding and not quite a cake, but something in between. As the dessert bakes, a light, spongy cake forms over a delicate bottom layer of custard. Lemon juice and lemon rind provide a double dose of tartness, but the berries keep sweetness in the balance. You may use blueberries or raspberries, if you prefer.

Irish Bread Pudding

Evaporated fat-free milk is a good staple item to keep in the pantry. We often use it in recipes such as soups and sauces because it adds a little more body and creaminess than regular fat-free milk. In this recipe, we used a combination of evaporated fat-free milk and 1% low-fat milk instead of cream. We kept the creamy, rich texture and flavor but got rid of most of the fat.

¼ cup light butter, melted
1 (10-ounce) French bread baguette, cut into 1-inch-thick slices
½ cup raisins
¼ cup Irish whiskey or ¼ cup apple juice
1¾ cups 1% low-fat milk
1 cup sugar
1 tablespoon vanilla extract
1 (12-ounce) can evaporated fat-free milk
2 large eggs, lightly beaten
Cooking spray
1 tablespoon sugar
1 teaspoon ground cinnamon
Caramel-Whiskey Sauce

1. Preheat oven to 350°.

2. Brush melted butter on one side of French bread slices; place bread slices, buttered sides up, on a baking sheet. Bake at 350° for 10 minutes or until lightly toasted. Cut bread into ½-inch cubes; set aside.

3. While bread is toasting, combine raisins and whiskey in a small bowl; cover and let stand 10 minutes or until soft (do not drain).

4. Combine 1% milk and next 4 ingredients in a large bowl; stir well with a whisk. Add bread cubes and raisin mixture, pressing gently to moisten, and let stand 15 minutes. Spoon bread mixture into a 13 x 9–inch baking dish coated with cooking spray. Combine 1 tablespoon sugar and cinnamon, and sprinkle over pudding. Bake at 350° for 35 minutes or until pudding is set. Serve warm with Caramel-Whiskey Sauce. Yield: 12 servings (serving size: 1 [3-inch] square and 2 tablespoons sauce).

(Totals include Caramel-Whiskey Sauce) CALORIES 360 (18% from fat); FAT 7.3g (sat 3.2g, mono 1.9g, poly 0.5g); PROTEIN 7.3g; CARB 65.9g; FIBER 1g; CHOL 57mg; IRON 1.1mg; SODIUM 275mg; CALC 164mg

Caramel-Whiskey Sauce

1½ cups sugar
⅔ cup water
¼ cup light butter
¼ cup (2 ounces) ⅓-less-fat cream cheese
¼ cup Irish whiskey
¼ cup 1% low-fat milk

1. Combine sugar and water in a small, heavy saucepan over medium-high heat; cook until sugar dissolves, stirring constantly. Cook 15 minutes or until golden (do not stir). Remove from heat. Carefully add butter and cream cheese, stirring constantly with a whisk (mixture will be hot and will bubble vigorously). Cool slightly, and stir in whiskey and milk. Yield: 1½ cups (serving size: 2 tablespoons).

Note: Substitute 1 tablespoon imitation rum extract and 3 tablespoons water for Irish whiskey, if desired.

CALORIES 138 (22% from fat); FAT 3.3g (sat 1.3g, mono 0.6g, poly 0.1g); PROTEIN 0.6g; CARB 25.9g; FIBER 0g; CHOL 11mg; IRON 0mg; SODIUM 45mg; CALC 11mg

Fudgy Mint Fallen Soufflé

½ cup boiling water
½ cup fresh mint leaves
⅔ cup unsweetened cocoa
2 tablespoons butter
3 tablespoons all-purpose flour
1 cup fat-free milk
½ cup granulated sugar
⅛ teaspoon salt
4 large egg whites
2 tablespoons granulated sugar
Cooking spray
1 tablespoon powdered sugar
Mint sprigs (optional)

1. Combine boiling water and mint leaves in a small bowl; cover and steep 20 minutes.

2. Preheat oven to 375°.

3. Strain mint mixture through a fine sieve into a large bowl; discard mint leaves. Add cocoa to water; stir well with a whisk.

4. Melt butter in a small saucepan over medium heat. Add flour, stirring with a whisk. Cook 1 minute, stirring constantly. Stir in milk, ½ cup granulated sugar, and salt; cook over medium heat 3 minutes or until thick, stirring constantly. Remove from heat, and stir into cocoa mixture. Cool slightly.

5. Place egg whites in a large bowl, and beat with a mixer at high speed until foamy. Add 2 tablespoons granulated sugar, 1 tablespoon at a time, beating until stiff peaks form. Gently stir one-fourth of egg white mixture into cocoa mixture; gently fold in remaining egg white mixture. Spoon into a 2-quart soufflé dish coated with cooking spray. Bake at 375° for 30 minutes or until puffy and set. Let stand 5 minutes (soufflé will fall during standing). Sprinkle with powdered sugar; garnish with mint sprigs, if desired. Serve warm or at room temperature. Yield: 6 servings (serving size: about ⅔ cup).

CALORIES 181 (26% from fat); FAT 5.2g (sat 2.7g, mono 2g, poly 0.2g); PROTEIN 6.1g; CARB 32.4g; FIBER 3.3g; CHOL 11mg; IRON 1.7mg; SODIUM 133mg; CALC 53mg

If you're buying mint at the market, look for bright green, crisp leaves with no signs of wilting. Place the stems in a glass containing a couple of inches of water, and cover the leaves loosely with plastic wrap or a zip-top plastic bag (do not seal the bag). Refrigerate up to one week, changing the water every other day. Fresh mint can also be frozen for later use. Simply rinse the leaves, pat them dry, and freeze them in a zip-top plastic bag (the leaves will darken once they're frozen, but that won't affect the flavor). Later, pull out what you need, and return the rest to the freezer.

Fresh mint leaves steep in hot water to create a mint "tea" that pairs with chocolate in this rich dessert. Because this soufflé is meant to be served fallen, there's no mad rush to get it to the table. As it deflates, the rich dessert becomes more dense and fudgy. For a special treat, serve vanilla ice cream on the side.

Hot Maple Soufflés

Correctly beating the egg whites is the key to a soufflé's success. Though eggs separate easier when they're cold, they beat to a greater volume at room temperature. To do both, separate your eggs while they're cold, and then let them sit while you gather the rest of the ingredients. Don't wait more than 30 minutes, though, for egg safety reasons.

1 tablespoon butter, softened
2 tablespoons granulated sugar
3 tablespoons bourbon
3 tablespoons maple syrup
1 cup maple syrup
4 large egg whites
⅛ teaspoon salt
1 teaspoon baking powder
1 tablespoon powdered sugar

1. Preheat oven to 425°.
2. Coat 6 (10-ounce) ramekins with butter, and sprinkle evenly with granulated sugar. Combine bourbon and 3 tablespoons syrup in a small microwave-safe bowl; microwave at HIGH 1½ minutes or until mixture boils. Pour about 1 tablespoon bourbon mixture into each prepared ramekin.
3. Cook 1 cup syrup in a medium, heavy saucepan over medium-high heat 8 minutes or until a candy thermometer registers 250°.
4. Beat egg whites and salt with a mixer at medium speed until foamy. Pour hot maple syrup in a thin stream over egg whites, beating at medium speed, then at high speed, until stiff peaks form. Add baking powder; beat well.
5. Spoon evenly into ramekins; place on a jelly-roll pan. Bake at 425° for 13 minutes or until puffy and set. Sprinkle with powdered sugar. Serve immediately. Yield: 6 servings (serving size: 1 soufflé).

CALORIES 212 (8% from fat); FAT 2g (sat 0.4g, mono 0.8g, poly 0.6g); PROTEIN 2.3g; CARB 47.8g; FIBER 0g; CHOL 0mg; IRON 0.8mg; SODIUM 193mg; CALC 89mg

Hot Maple Soufflés have become a holiday favorite at Cooking Light. The ingredients are simple, but the technique elevates the soufflés—literally and figuratively. The richness of maple syrup is added to these soufflés without weighing them down with fat and calories. By boiling syrup with bourbon, the flavors are concentrated for an intensity that memorably contrasts with the soufflés' airy texture. They taste like pancakes in maple syrup.

all about
Dessert

Simple or spectacular, dessert is often the highlight of a meal. And since desserts take on many shapes, our recipes require a wide variety of ingredients, equipment, and special techniques.

A Well-Tooled Kitchen

Before you begin creating dazzling desserts, you'll want to make sure that your kitchen is well stocked with the necessary tools. With the correct cookware, utensils, and equipment, you'll discover that you can create luscious, healthy desserts that rival those of professional chefs.

Cookware

Dessert cookware consists of baking pans, pots and pans, and assorted glass dishes—all of which are crucial for making stellar desserts. Using the right cookware helps create tender cakes, fluffy soufflés, and creamy puddings. So how do you know how to pick the right cookware? Here's a quick guide to the pans we use most often.

• *Baking Sheet* Also called a cookie sheet, a baking sheet is a flat pan with a low rim on one or two ends, or low rims on all four sides with open corners for air circulation. They're designed for sliding cookies onto a wire rack. You can buy baking sheets with nonstick surfaces or insulated sheets. Insulated sheets bake cookies a little slower than the nonstick pans.

• *Jelly-Roll Pan* A jelly-roll pan is a 15 x 10–inch pan that's used to make thin cakes, such as sponge cakes and jelly-rolls. It's sometimes called a sheet pan, and it has a rim on all four sides and closed corners. Jelly-roll pans come with both shiny and dark finishes and may have nonstick surfaces.

• *Tube Pan* The 10-inch tube pan, also called an angel food cake pan, is a classic tall-sided, round cake pan with a tube in the center. Sometimes it has a removable center; sometimes it doesn't. Some types have small metal feet on the top rim so you can turn them upside down for cooling. If your pan doesn't have feet and your recipe tells you to "hang" the cake upside down to cool, as many angel food cake recipes do, you can invert it on a bottle with a long neck.

• *Springform Pan* A springform pan is a round, deep pan with tall, removable sides; it's most often used for baking cheesecakes. Springform pans with glass bottoms conduct heat better and decrease baking time, and those with extended edges around the base keep the batter from leaking. Nine-inch pans are the most popular. If your springform pan isn't the size called for in the recipe, you can use a smaller one, but your cake will be thicker and may need to bake longer. Conversely, if you use a larger pan than the recipe calls for, your cake will be thinner and may require less baking time.

Utensils

From can openers to measuring cups and spoons, and from whisks to kitchen shears, utensils are a must-have in any dessert-lover's kitchen.

Whisks come in assorted sizes and are ideal for beating eggs and egg whites. They are excellent for stirring custards.

You can cover an array of kitchen tasks with just three knifes: a chef's knife, a serrated knife, and a paring knife. Each has functions unique to its shape and design.

A large *chef's knife* is best used for chopping ingredients such as nuts, fruits, or chocolate. A *serrated knife* is ideal for slicing delicate angel food cakes and jelly

rolls or hard-crusted biscotti. A *paring knife* is best used for peeling fruits, cutting shapes or vents for dough, sectioning an orange, or slicing bar cookies in the pan. See our checklist on the following page for a complete list of kitchen utensils to keep on hand.

Other Equipment

Small electric appliances also make preparing desserts easier for any cook. Here are our suggestions for appliances we consider necessities:

• *Blender* For some recipes, a blender actually does a better job of combining the ingredients than a food processor. This piece of kitchen equipment is ideal for blending blueberries and blueberry preserves in Blueberry Gelato (recipe on page 112).

• *Food Processor* A food processor can make speedy work out of slicing and chopping fruits, blending ingredients, and kneading dough. The dough for Coffee-Hazelnut Biscotti (recipe on

page 42) comes together quickly using a food processor. Food processors come in different sizes to accommodate different amounts of food, and most come with a set of blades for different tasks, such as shredding and slicing.

• *Microwave Oven* Most people seem to use microwave ovens only to reheat leftovers or steam vegetables. But a microwave, in our opinion, has far greater uses. Our Test Kitchens use the microwave as a shortcut when melting butter and chocolate, toasting nuts, and heating milk. It's also a quick and easy way to defrost frozen fruits.

• *Stand Mixer* Stand mixers are good for mixing large amounts of batter and heavy batters. The recipes in this book can be prepared using a stand or heavy-duty mixer. Heavy-duty mixers (such as KitchenAid) are designed like commercial mixers, with a single paddle and a powerful motor. "Heavy-duty" means they can handle thick dough, such as

cookie dough, without burning up the motor. The bowls on them are large, which is very helpful when you have large amounts of batter or dough. They usually come with multiple attachments, such as whisks for beating egg whites or whipping cream, a paddle for creaming butter and sugar, and dough hooks for kneading bread. An especially nice thing about these mixers is that the dough does not crawl up the beaters like it does with other mixers, especially when you have a thick dough. Generally, we only call for heavy-duty mixers for thick batters or for kneading breads.

• *Handheld Mixers* Handheld mixers are fine for mixing most batters. They are small, easy to store, and offer great control. When you're using this type of mixer, you don't have to stop and scrape down the sides of the bowl. However, these small mixers will not be able to handle thick cake or cookie batter.

Kitchen Equipment Checklist

Here is a list of the essential kitchen equipment that is necessary for making desserts. It's certainly not a complete list, but it's a good start for the basics. If you have these items in your kitchen, you should be able to make any dessert in this book.

Assorted baking pans
- ❑ Baking sheet
- ❑ Jelly-roll, 15 x 10–inch
- ❑ Loaf
- ❑ Muffin
- ❑ Round cake, 8- and 9-inch
- ❑ Springform, 7-, 8-, and 9-inch
- ❑ Square, 8- and 9-inch
- ❑ 13 x 9–inch
- ❑ Tart (round, removable-bottom)
- ❑ Tube, 10-inch
- ❑ Wire rack

Pots and pans
- ❑ Dutch oven: 3- to 6-quart
- ❑ Heavy saucepans
  - ❑ small (1½-quart)
  - ❑ medium (2-quart)
  - ❑ large (3-quart)
- ❑ Nonstick skillets:
  - ❑ 10-inch
  - ❑ 12-inch
  - ❑ cast-iron skillet
- ❑ Roasting pan (for water bath)

Assorted glass dishes
- ❑ Baking dishes, 11 x 7– and 13 x 9–inch
- ❑ Pie plate, 9- and 10-inch
- ❑ Custard cups
- ❑ Regular and individual soufflé dishes

Utensils
- ❑ Can opener
- ❑ Colander, strainer, and sieve
- ❑ Corkscrew

- ❑ Graters: box and handheld
- ❑ Handheld juicer
- ❑ Heatproof spatula
- ❑ Metal icing spatula
- ❑ Kitchen shears or scissors
- ❑ Measuring cups
  - ❑ dry and liquid
- ❑ Measuring spoons
- ❑ Pastry blender
- ❑ Potato masher
- ❑ Rolling pin
- ❑ Thermometers
  - ❑ instant-read
  - ❑ oven
  - ❑ candy
- ❑ Vegetable peeler
- ❑ Whisk
- ❑ Wooden and slotted spoons
- ❑ Melon baller
- ❑ Cookie scoops
- ❑ Ice cream scoop
- ❑ Biscuit cutter, 3-inch
- ❑ Basting brush

Other equipment
- ❑ Cutting boards
- ❑ Blender
- ❑ Food processor
- ❑ Food scale
- ❑ Glass mixing bowls
- ❑ Handheld electric mixer
- ❑ Pepper mill
- ❑ Stand mixer
- ❑ Ice cream freezer
- ❑ Kitchen torch

Essential Techniques for Measuring

Measuring ingredients when preparing desserts is very important. It can mean the difference between a prize-winning delight and a disappointing disaster.

Creating healthy, scrumptious desserts depends on adding just the right amount of ingredients. Get in the habit of measuring with precision. Liquid and dry ingredients are measured using different techniques and utensils.

Dry Ingredients

In general, healthy recipes call for less fat than traditional recipes. When fat is reduced in baking, the precise measurement of flour becomes crucial. Too much flour results in a very dry product. How you measure flour can make a huge difference—as much as an ounce per cup. If flour is scooped out of the canister with the measuring cup, it's likely that too much flour will be used. Therefore, correctly measuring flour is extremely important when making light recipes. Specific directions for measuring flour are included with recipes that call for ¼ cup or more of flour.

How to Measure Flour

1. Rather than scooping the flour out of the canister or bag, fluff the flour with a fork. Then lightly spoon the flour into a dry measuring cup without compacting it. Scooping the flour can add up to 3½ tablespoons per cup too much flour.

2. Level the top of the flour with a knife or a straight edge to get an even cup, scraping excess back into the canister.

Liquid Ingredients

When measuring liquid ingredients, always use a liquid measuring cup so you can see the exact measurement through the side of the cup. If you measure liquid ingredients in a dry measuring cup, you may add too much or too little liquid. After you pour in the liquid, check the amount at eye level. Or use a liquid measuring cup with an angled surface that allows you to look down into the cup and read the measurement correctly.

No-Stick Measuring

If you're measuring honey, molasses, or peanut butter for a recipe that also includes oil, measure the oil first. The oil will coat the inside so that the sweetener won't stick to the cup. Or coat the inside of a measuring cup with cooking spray first before measuring the sticky ingredient.

Essential Techniques for Making the Perfect Pastry

A classic piecrust requires the right combination of butter and shortening and the best proportion of flour to ice water. Use the following piecrust recipe and step-by-step instructions to make the perfect pastry.

Piecrust

This recipe makes a 9- or 10-inch crust that's much tastier than commercial pie dough. This dough can be rolled out and frozen between sheets of plastic wrap for up to a week, or rolled out, placed in a pie plate, covered tightly, and refrigerated for two days.

1½ cups all-purpose flour
2 tablespoons sugar
¼ teaspoon salt
3 tablespoons butter
2 tablespoons vegetable
  shortening
4 tablespoons ice water
Cooking spray

1. Lightly spoon flour into dry measuring cups; level with a knife. Combine flour, sugar, and salt in a bowl; cut in butter and shortening with a pastry blender or 2 knives until mixture resembles coarse meal. Sprinkle surface with ice water, 1 tablespoon at a time; toss with a fork until moist and crumbly (do not form a ball).
2. Press mixture into a 4-inch circle on plastic wrap; cover and chill 15 minutes. Slightly overlap sheets of plastic wrap on a damp surface. Unwrap and place chilled dough on plastic wrap. Cover with 2 additional sheets of overlapping plastic wrap. Roll dough, still covered, into a 13-inch circle. Place dough in

freezer 5 minutes or until plastic wrap can easily be removed.
3. Preheat oven to 400°.
4. Remove top sheets of plastic wrap; fit dough, plastic wrap side up, into a pie plate coated with cooking spray. Remove remaining plastic wrap. Fold edges under, and flute. Pierce bottom and sides of dough with a fork; bake at 400° for 15 minutes. Cool on a wire rack. Yield: 1 piecrust (10 servings).

CALORIES 113 (48% from fat); FAT 6g (sat 2.7g, mono 2.1g, poly 0.8g); PROTEIN 1.8g; CARB 13g; FIBER 0.5g; CHOL 9mg; IRON 0.8mg; SODIUM 65mg; CALC 1mg

2. Press dough into a 4-inch circle on plastic wrap; cover and chill 15 minutes. Slightly overlap sheets of plastic wrap on a damp surface. Unwrap and place chilled dough on plastic wrap. Cover with 2 additional sheets of overlapping plastic wrap.

1. Cutting in the fat with a pastry blender (or with two knives) is a process that combines flour, butter, and shortening until the mixture resembles coarse meal. This technique evenly distributes the fat throughout the flour, making a flaky pastry.

3. Roll dough, still covered, into a 13-inch circle. To get an even thickness, try rolling north, south, east, and west. Lift up the rolling pin as you near the edges so they won't get too thin. Place dough in freezer 5 minutes or until plastic wrap can easily be removed.

Essential Techniques for Making Layer Cakes

Layer cakes from scratch are not only tastier than cakes from a box, they're also surprisingly easy.
A stand mixer (a handheld mixer also will work), a rubber spatula, cake pans, and
wax paper are the basic pieces of equipment you need.

1. In low-fat baking, pans are not heavily greased, so for some cake recipes, we line pans with wax paper to make sure the cake doesn't stick. Using the baking pan as a template, cut the paper to fit the inside of the pans. Coat the bottoms of the pans with cooking spray; line with wax paper. Coat the wax paper with cooking spray; dust with flour.

2. Before measuring, stir the flour to make sure there aren't any lumps. Measure flour accurately. Lightly spoon it into a dry measuring cup, and level it with a knife. Don't scoop—you'll get too much flour, and the cake will be dry.

3. When you beat the shortening and sugar together (traditionally called creaming) for a low-fat cake, the mixture will not look creamy and fluffy as in a traditional cake recipe. Instead, the consistency will be more like damp sand—fine-textured, but not cohesive.

4. Add the eggs and the egg whites to the batter one at a time, beating each one thoroughly before adding the next.

5. Add the flour mixture alternately with the liquid, as you would with any cake. Beat just until each component is incorporated. Overbeating at this stage can produce a tough cake.

6. When frosting the cake, first brush away any loose crumbs. Tear off four strips of wax paper; place them in a square on the cake plate. Place a cake layer on top of the strips. Frost the cake.

Frostings

Frostings help round out most cake recipes, and these fabulous additions are certainly no exception: Our Coconut-Pecan Frosting goes with German Chocolate Cake (recipe on page 66), while Fluffy Coconut Frosting tops off Coconut Triple-Layer Cake (recipe on page 68).

Coconut-Pecan Frosting

  2 tablespoons butter
⅓ cup finely chopped pecans
⅔ cup packed brown sugar
  2 tablespoons cornstarch
¼ teaspoon salt
  1 cup fat-free sweetened
      condensed milk
  1 tablespoon light-colored corn
      syrup
  2 large egg yolks
½ cup flaked sweetened coconut,
      toasted
2½ teaspoons vanilla extract
⅛ teaspoon coconut extract

1. Melt butter in a medium saucepan over medium-high heat. Add chopped pecans, and sauté until pecans are browned (about 2½ minutes). Remove from heat, and stir in sugar, cornstarch, and salt. Add milk, syrup, and egg yolks, stir well. Cook over medium-high heat 2 minutes or until thick, stirring constantly. Remove from heat, and stir in flaked coconut and extracts. Pour into a bowl; cover and chill until slightly stiff (about 15 minutes). Yield: 2 cups (serving size: 1 tablespoon).

CALORIES 77 (29% from fat); FAT 2.5g (sat 1.1g, mono 0.9g, poly 0.3g); PROTEIN 1.1g; CARB 12.4g; FIBER 0.2g; CHOL 16mg; IRON 0.2mg; SODIUM 35mg; CALC 31mg

Fluffy Coconut Frosting

  1 cup sugar
¼ cup water
¼ teaspoon cream of tartar
Dash of salt
  3 large egg whites
  1 teaspoon vanilla extract
¼ teaspoon coconut extract

1. Combine first 5 ingredients in top of a double boiler; cook over simmering water, beating with a mixer at high speed until stiff peaks form and a candy thermometer registers 160° (about 7 minutes). Add extracts; beat until well blended. Yield: 4 cups (serving size: 1 tablespoon).

CALORIES 13 (0% from fat); FAT 0g; PROTEIN 0.2g; CARB 3.2g; FIBER 0g; CHOL 0mg; IRON 0mg; SODIUM 5mg; CALC 0mg

7 Tips for Great Low-Fat Cookies

Here are our Test Kitchens staffers' tips for making cookies that melt in your mouth:

1. Measure flour correctly; too much flour will make the cookies tough (see page 138 for how to measure).

2. If the batter seems dry, don't give in to the temptation to add more liquid. This makes for a cakelike cookie that spreads too much.

3. Use the exact ingredients called for in the recipe. Baking cookies is like conducting a science experiment because both the right balance and type of ingredients are crucial.

4. Use real butter unless the recipe specifically calls for light butter. Do not use margarine or any whipped or spreadable butters.

5. Cookies bake more evenly when they're about the same size. And don't forget that they need plenty of space between them to allow for spreading.

6. We bake cookies on the second rack from the bottom of the oven. Be sure there is room left for air to circulate on all sides after the baking sheet is placed on the rack.

7. Bake cookies in an oven that has been preheated for 15 minutes. Check for doneness at the earliest suggested time. Opening and closing the oven door too often can change baking times.

Subject Index

Recipe Index